The Military Leader

Fundamental Insight for Developing Leaders

ANDREW STEADMAN

WESTBOW
PRESS®
A DIVISION OF THOMAS NELSON
& ZONDERVAN

The views expressed here do not represent the Department of Defense or the United States Government in any way.

WestBow Press books may be ordered through booksellers or by contacting:

WestBow Press
A Division of Thomas Nelson & Zondervan
1663 Liberty Drive
Bloomington, IN 47403
www.westbowpress.com
1 (866) 928-1240

ISBN: 978-1-9736-2899-6 (sc)
ISBN: 978-1-9736-2900-9 (hc)
ISBN: 978-1-9736-2898-9 (e)

Library of Congress Control Number: 2018905925

Print information available on the last page.

WestBow Press rev. date: 11/21/2018

Dedication

For AG, LB, and my Em.

Epigraph

"Everything rises and falls on leadership."
~ John C. Maxwell

Contents

Sharpen Your Skills

Grow Your Team

Foreword by General David G. Perkins, U.S. Army Retired

In every organization I have seen, the one essential "secret sauce" needed for success is leadership. On every battlefield, in every trench and command post, in ship bridges and aircraft cockpits, men and women have exercised leadership as a necessary means to inspire and drive people towards success.

I have witnessed this fact throughout my 38-year Army career. As a young officer, I benefitted from the leadership of a great young NCO who developed and inspired my leadership style that stayed with me for my entire career in both peace and combat. Decades later in the attack on Baghdad, I saw how great leadership overcame every obstacle put in a unit's way, like blinding dust storms, being highly outnumbered by the enemy, an enemy that was far more familiar with the terrain and environment, and a lack of fuel and repair parts. The only thing going for us was that we 'out-led' everybody we came in contact with. Finally, as the Commanding General of the Army's Training and Doctrine Command, I observed the mentorship and professional leadership displayed by instructors and trainers charged with making the Army ready for war and that the institutionalization of developing leaders at all levels is what sets our military apart from all others.

As Andrew states in this book, "Leadership is everywhere people are. It is the element that converts the potential energy of our organizations into mission accomplishment. Without quality leadership, we fail."

This is true for the seasoned General as well as the newest Private. I found I had more learning and growing to do as a four star general to meet the

Army's expectations than I did as a newly commissioned Lieutenant. Every member of our military must cultivate the ability to lead, and to lead you must also know how to follow. Leadership must be a primary field of study with daily practice and growth, not simply the accumulation of lessons born out of experience. There is too much at stake to do otherwise.

For the last 20 years, Andrew Steadman has made leadership his professional and personal passion. With the combat theaters of Iraq and Afghanistan as proving grounds, he has discovered what it takes build great leaders. From character to combat mindset, counseling to change of command speeches, *The Military Leader* is a compendium of advice, lessons, and inspiration with a single purpose…to grow leaders.

You will find that *The Military Leader* offers a constant challenge to improve yourself as a leader. Andrew's creative methods for simple events like counseling are enriching, but you need not embark on a holistic remake of your leadership approach. I encourage you to highlight a technique here and there and adapt it for the type of leader you are and the team you lead. Don't overthink it, just commit to steady improvement.

Importantly, leadership is timeless, universal, and situation non-dependent. Businesses, non-profits, and private sector organizations will find that *The Military Leader* is a powerful dose of the stuff that makes military leaders so effective. Yet, it is also highly relevant and applicable for non-military leadership. I have found the most consequential and enduring leadership impacts occur when you least expect them and when they are personally internalized. Consider this excerpt, which characterizes Andrew's insight throughout the book:

> "Leaders influence followers in ways that are often less-direct and more personal. Just as you have chosen what talents you like about your leaders, your followers get to choose what traits they will model after you. Each person views your leadership from a different perspective and a different set of needs. Some are looking for perseverance during busy times. Others are disgruntled and need the passion reignited. Some need a good lesson in humility.

Still others will bend their parenting behavior to model your character traits.

You don't get to decide which lessons people take from your example or when they decide to learn from your behavior. You're always 'on' and you will likely never discover the true impact of your leadership. This is both the burden and the blessing of leadership...make it count."

Indeed, powerful for all professions.

Finally, I am excited about *The Military Leader* because it represents a growing trend that is emerging in our military: influencing beyond the chain of command. More and more active duty leaders are contributing their insight in the form of blogs, podcasts, forums, books, and social media. In doing so, they extend their influence beyond the boundaries of their assigned unit or team.

The Strategy Bridge, Small Wars Journal, Modern War Institute, From the Green Notebook, 3x5 Leadership, Company Grade Leader, Field Grade Leader, Leader's Huddle Podcast, The Military Leader Podcast, and the Defense Entrepreneur's Forum are among many others you should consider.

This grassroots professional growth is encouraging, for not only does it add personal perspective to augment formal leader development programs, but it encourages growing leaders to contribute their own lessons for others to draw upon. And as we look to the future of military leadership in a fast-paced, complex world, the ability to grow rapidly will be an indispensable quality.

The opportunity to lead is truly a gift and a heavy reasonability. I am confident that *The Military Leader* will become a cornerstone resource on your journey to becoming a more effective and influential leader.

Acknowledgments

The leaders and readers who make up The Military Leader community have made this book possible. I am humbled and excited by every person who writes to say that the content added value. Thanks to everyone who has made The Military Leader a part of your day.

I am lucky to have had mentors who selflessly invested their time, energy, and patience into shaping my own leader development. Among them are Brian Berry, Dan Fisher, Don McCreary, Greg Scott, Dale Condit, Jeff Kozyra, Marty Schweitzer, Lou Zeisman, Pete Johnson, Greg Cannata, D.A. Sims, Jim Isenhower, Omar Jones, Robert Brown, Chris Keller, Dan Barnett, Matt Broaddus, Mike McMurphy, Jon Byrom, John B. Richardson IV, Scott O'Neal, Mark Milley, Paul Norwood, Jasper Jeffers, and Ross Coffman.

Many, many Non-Commissioned Officers along the way were instrumental in balancing my notions of leadership with the reality of life in the enlisted ranks. Most notably, Chuck McManus, Rudi Soto, Jim Champagne, Steve Lewis, Andy Almueti, Mike Boom, Chuck Owens, Scott Schroeder, Terry Weiss, and Mike Luther are NCO leaders I am thankful for.

Sharing the leadership journey are many friends with whom I have come to rely on for advice, insight, and support, especially Bryan Raridon, Dan Courtright, Mark Michalek, Javier Lopez, Anthony Randall, Matt Rasmussen, Justin Uhler, Jeff Barta, Corey Landry, Noble Gibbens, Tim Gatlin, Rob Stanton, Cory Sullivan, Adam Lackey, Wes Spurlock, Stephen Dobbins, Sean Lucas, Adisa King, Scott Shaw, Rob Shaw, Charles Ford, Matt Albertus, Les Minges, and Matt Hardman.

Since starting The Military Leader, I've come to know many exceptionally talented professionals who are growing the force through their own writing. Some I know only through Twitter, but we share ideas, edit each other's work, and highlight one another's content. I am especially grateful for Joe Byerly, Nate Finney, Steve Leonard, Doug Meyer, Josh Powers, Jessica Dawson, Angry Staff Officer, Mick Ryan, Phil Walter, Josh Bowen, and David Weart.

Bev Weiler had the laborious task of editing this manuscript and I thank her for her enduring patience and meticulous eye.

The idea to write this book came from friend, officer, and fellow creative Steve Pugh. Without his encouragement, it would not exist.

Finally, my family has been wonderfully supportive and I especially thank Emily and the girls for selflessly granting me the space to pursue this lifelong goal of publishing a book. You're my people. Mom and Dad, thank you for always being proud, regardless of the result.

Introduction

It was Monday morning and this was the first encounter of the day with the Captains and Lieutenants of the Operations Section. I was their leader, the Operations Officer of the 3d Cavalry Regiment at Fort Hood, Texas. I had stepped into a key moment in my career — and in the unit's long history stretching back to 1846 — and I was well on my way to having no appreciable impact on the people I was charged to lead and inspire.

Lost in the battle rhythm of a modern-day US Army unit, I had become a task manager. Instead of asking my team how their weekend went or how their Soldiers were doing, I instead jumped right to the status, timeline, and task updates that represent the mundane parts of running an organization.

I was not connecting with my followers on a personal level as their leader, let alone as a mentor, and I was dangerously close to becoming one of those leaders who breeze through a unit with much success, but little impact. Yes, it is possible to do an outstanding job for the organization but do a terrible job growing the people who make up that organization.

Then, thanks to timely advice from a trusted mentor, I had an awakening.

I realized that I should be doing more for my team. They wanted more than to show up to work and simply get the job done. They wanted to be led with passion, ingenuity, inspiration, and concern for their personal and professional lives. They were eager to learn how to become leaders themselves, fulfill their goals in the Army, and (dare I say) to find their life's purpose.

Who better or more responsible to create that environment than their leader?

So, I started my course correction by telling them exactly what was on my mind. "Guys, if we're not careful, the 'busyness' of this place will get the best of all of us and we'll walk out of here no better than when we came in." I committed to connecting with them in ways that stretched beyond the routine tasks. I promised that in addition to running the organization, we would focus on leader development and do what I had affirmed in the past but forgotten: to grow leaders instead of just better followers.

The unit leadership was already building tactical warfighting knowledge, but we chose to complement that program by exploring nonmilitary leadership content. Our research took us to publications like *Harvard Business Review*, *FastCompany*, and *Inc. Magazine*; authors like John Maxwell, Malcolm Gladwell, Stephen Covey, Jim Collins, and Marshall Goldsmith; podcasters like Michael Hyatt, Dave Ramsey, and Tim Ferriss; and to a library of powerful TED Talks.

The results were refreshing, insightful, and inspirational. Not only were we hitting the tip of an iceberg of nonmilitary leader development, we were honing our ability to *develop ourselves* instead of waiting on "experience" to do it for us. And we took away professional, ethical, and moral lessons that will echo through our careers.

Twelve months later I had another insight, *"I'm probably not the only military leader who has struggled to connect with his team in a meaningful way."* I figured there were countless leaders out there looking for ways to have lasting impact. *"How could I share that hard-earned leader development process with the force? What if those leader development resources and insights existed in one place for leaders to quickly access and use?"*

As if on cue, I happened across Michael Hyatt's tutorial, "How to set up your WordPress blog in 20 minutes" and I was all in.

Since the first post in March 2014, **millions of people** have made The Military Leader website a part of their leadership development. The recent additions of a podcast and webinar series are reaching even more people. I am humbled and ecstatic that leaders find value in the content and use it to have a positive effect on their teams. To me, that's mission accomplished!

This book is a continuation of that effort and fulfills a request made by many people to publish the lessons in a form that is standalone, easy to reference, and shareable. Each chapter covers a separate topic area, so there's no need to read the book sequentially. You can jump around to find the content that is most relevant for you.

The concept is straightforward: Grow yourself then grow your team.

Section 1 encourages leaders to nurture a curiosity for leadership and embark on a personal development program that will build a foundation of leadership skills. Section 2 helps leaders develop the day-to-day skills that will help them become effective and efficient leaders. Section 3 is all about connecting with and growing those around you to become better leaders themselves.

I want to emphasize is that great leadership is not a default state. You must fight to intentionally acquire new insight, skills, personality traits, and character facets that turn you into the leader your people deserve. I offer *The Military Leader* as a resource to help you achieve that excellence. Thanks for making it a part of your leadership journey!

Lead well,

Drew

Section 1

Grow Yourself

How Do You Spot a Leader?

Leaders must behave differently than those they lead. They were picked for a certain job because their personalities or abilities surpassed those around them and they could be counted on to make a difference. Analyze your own leadership traits in light of these questions:

If an outsider were to look in on your organization without explanation or even the ability to hear what was going on, would they be able to tell that you are the leader? What traits would they be looking for to explain who is in charge?

No need to answer in public, but consider the following as traits leaders must display if they are to make a difference in the organization.

Leaders...

Do Things First — Leaders are the ones who should apply the mental energy to come up with new ideas, try out different techniques, and create innovative solutions. They are the first to volunteer in tackling a challenging or dangerous situation. Leaders make things happen by doing, not by watching.

Are the Source of Energy — In case you haven't realized it, the energy your followers apply to their jobs is directly tied to your enthusiasm for the mission, your passion for the organization's purpose, and **your ability to communicate both**.

Inspiration does not have a duty-day. Soldiers will need to see your internal drive despite the fact that it's 0200, cold, raining, and miserable. They will look to your example as a measure of "performance expectation." And if you aren't getting after it, you can almost guarantee that they won't be, either. Never forget, the energy comes from YOU!

Move Faster Than Everyone Else — If you are a leader and you find yourself moving slowly throughout the day, you are probably not doing enough to help out the team. Read what John Maxwell in *The 360° Leader* says about the speed of leaders:

> Though it is not always true, in general the higher you go in an organization's hierarchy, the faster the leaders travel. The leader at the top often has boundless energy and is very quick mentally. Conversely, when you move down, people move more slowly. Generally, people at the bottom don't process information as quickly, and they don't make decisions as fast. Part of that is due to having less information. Some of it comes from having less experience. Most people who want to lead are naturally fast.

Most of the time, leaders dart from one event to the next, or are focusing to create a new product/presentation that will help the team. They are always looking to identify problems in the organization and tackle them quickly, so that the organization can become better or more effective.

They can also switch topics rapidly, adjusting leadership sets to accommodate varying situations. This is especially important for us as Army leaders, as we often have to deal with operations one minute, then switch to family problems the next, then wrap-up by developing a long-range supply plan. To do this, you have to be fast.

Solve Their Followers' Problems —

> *Leadership is solving problems. The day your*
> *soldiers stop bringing you their*
> *problems is the day you've stopped leading them.*
> ~ General Colin Powell, *My American Journey*

How very true. Soldiers develop trust when they genuinely feel that you care about their problems, won't blow up and crush them for having problems, and will be committed to helping solve them. Without that confidence, the Soldier might as well be in a different unit.

Helping solve their issues empowers you as a leader in two ways: one, you show your subordinates that you have the competence to get things done; and two, you build confidence that you will be there for them when they really need you, like in combat.

When the bullets are flying and the Soldier is scared out of his mind, he won't care about the fact that you went through Ranger School five years ago or that you can score 330 on your PT test. He will only care about how much you can help him get through that moment alive. **And if you've never helped him out before, he certainly won't expect you to save him when it matters**.

So, the questions stands … Could an outsider spot you, the leader, in your organization?

Why Curiosity Matters

I don't know about you, but I have noticed that the best leaders are always moving forward. They don't stagnate, are curious about themselves and their environment, and continually break new ground. They advance their talents intellectually, physically, emotionally, professionally, and so on.

When you think about it, curiosity is required before one can improve at all; it is a prerequisite for growth.

What Does Your Curiosity Reveal About You?

Your curiosity communicates certain aspects of who you are as a leader or member of a team. Having a hungry mind shows that:

You are willing to learn.
You aren't afraid to admit that what you have isn't enough.
You have energy to actively improve.
You can bring new skills to the organization.
You realize that the environment is changing and you need to adapt.

What Should You Be Curious About?

As military professionals responsible for the safety of our service members and the success of the mission, there are some areas in which you have a professional obligation to be curious, such as:

- Your current duty position
- Your own strengths, weaknesses, and methods you use to improve

- The lives, interests, concerns, motivations, and vulnerabilities of those you lead and work with
- The application of your particular skillset in combat (i.e., leading Infantry troops, supporting with logistics, maintaining digital connectivity, etc.)
- The capabilities of the enemies you are likely to face

Areas in which you should *develop* a professional curiosity include:

- Your next duty position
- Your boss's scope of responsibility, areas of concern, and requirements for achieving the unit's vision
- The historical significance of your unit and branch of service, which will give perspective and importance to your mission
- The military as a profession, particularly in the areas of ethics, civil–military relations, and the role of the military in society

What Does a Curious Leader Look Like?

Simply put: She reads, takes notes, engages in meaningful dialogue, and asks questions. The curious leader studies history and applies it to today. She integrates lessons from tangential professions to improve her skills and is open to new ideas. She does not accept "the way we've always done it" and continually seeks a better method. The curious leader is the one who is constantly growing, while others are content with staying in place.

Being "Somebody" Isn't Good Enough

"I always wanted to be somebody,
but I should have been more specific."
~ Lily Tomlin

We can draw some insightful leadership lessons from an unlikely source in Lily Tomlin. Her pithy quote certainly resonates to each of our personal ambitions, as it is dangerously easy to get sucked into passing the milestones of life without clearly defining where those milestones will lead, or the type of person we will become along the path.

Similarly, new Privates and Lieutenants step into active duty as proverbial blank slates, ready to combine real-world experience with the second-hand, academic, and imagined impressions they have of military service. Most have goals in mind, some vision of what "success" looks like for their time in service. Some want to be generals, some prioritize getting a college education, others are just happy to have survived Basic Training.

But how many service members—these future leaders—take their vision beyond a rank or position and specify the *type of leader* they want to be, and then outline *how* they plan to develop those skills throughout their career to reach that end state?

Like a Stick in a River

"I always wanted to be somebody, but I should have been more specific." There's a feeling of regret that underlies the humor of this quote. It's a realization that without intentionality, **life will direct our personal growth**

along paths of least resistance to arrive at a place that falls short of our potential. The same goes for professional and leader development.

The good news is that you have control over this process:

- You choose *when* to start defining the leader you will become.
- You filter *who* you surround yourself with to shape your development as a leader (friends, peers, mentors).
- You choose *what* inputs will define your growth (books, classes, movies, etc.).
- You direct the *quality* of your thoughts, which shape your outlook and attitudes.
- You commit to the *habits* that will shape who you become.
- You control your *response* to the world when it doesn't conform to your ambitions.

If the default "somebody" isn't good enough for you, you must take action:

- Read and study leaders that resonate with you.
- Ask mentors how they grew into their leader personas.
- Take notes about the leadership qualities you want to develop, as well as those you want to avoid.
- Identify the attitudes and behaviors that will define you as a leader. Will you be impulsive or deliberate? Charismatic or stoic? Demonstrative or subtle? Articulate and refined, or simple and relatable?
- Ask your peers, family, friends, bosses, and subordinates to help keep you on track.

Make sure your quote ends up being: "I always wanted to be somebody … *and this is who it is.*"

A Simple Observation About Great Leaders

One day in a conversation with a good friend, I realized that almost every time we get together, we end up talking about some professional development topic, usually leadership. I made a quick mental comparison of him with colleagues I had worked with over the years and concluded that my friend is a superbly talented leader, which brought an obvious insight into focus:

Great leaders regularly talk about leadership.
Leadership, for them, is at the very least a dedicated hobby,
but more often it is a passion.

Thinking back to the leaders and mentors I'd had, I found the principle to be true. The exceptional leaders continually engaged with others about leadership, making it a part of their daily purpose. It was as if they used discussion to develop, test, refine, and teach their own leadership styles.

Incorporating leadership topics into routine conversations has a number of effects:

- It reminds you that you are a leader.
- It forces you to formalize your beliefs as a leader.
- Discussion associates disconnected thoughts into new ideas and insights.
- It shows others that you are dedicated to your role as a leader.
- It inspires others to think about leadership.
- Talking about leadership communicates your intent to your colleagues and subordinates.

There is plenty of writing to support the assertion that the quality of your conversations significantly affects your thinking, your attitude, and ultimately the talents you can provide to followers. If you care about growing as a leader, pay close attention that you do so several times throughout each day, particularly in your conversations with other leaders.

In Leadership, You Are a Consumer, a Producer or Irrelevant

Consider this framework for thinking about personal development as a leader. It's a *"Lead, follow, or get out of the way"* approach that shines the spotlight on the personal habits that grow leaders into positions of effectiveness.

Here you go:

> When it comes to personal leadership development,
> you are a content consumer, a content producer ... or irrelevant.

Growth – the Seed of Influence

Personal leadership development is the combination of activities, interactions, and thought refinement that improves a leader's ability to create effects in his sphere of influence. Personal reading and participating in organizational leader development programs are certainly part of this process. But so is writing, engaging with peers and mentors, and introspectively sharpening one's own leadership beliefs. These activities make up some portion of the leader's day to create habits that **move the needle towards effectiveness and away from stagnation.**

Effective leaders have some balance of content consumption and production. They seek leadership insight from books, articles, and the people around them. They ask questions to drive their growth. They contemplate and refine their own leadership talents; then they use the resulting growth to produce positive effects in those around them. They talk about their own leadership journey, perhaps through professional writing. They apply the lessons they learn and share resources. They are a catalyst for leader development.

It's possible to be a consumer but not a producer (think about the quiet bookworm who never leaves the office or a follower who fails to pass on what he learns from his leaders.. But producers—that is, people who generate positive impact—are rarely absent some component of leadership consumption in their lives. **They know that quality input fuels meaningful output and they shape their habits accordingly.** (In light of this, the debate about whether or not leaders are "born or made" is irrelevant. *Better* leaders are definitely made.)

But those who choose to neither consume leader development content nor pass on practical lessons to others are irrelevant. **They don't move the ball down the field and they don't become better players.** They are often characterized by the proclamation, *"I rely on my experience to get the job done."* With respect to leadership, they are holes in the organization, perhaps even a drain to those who are really carrying the team forward.

Which Camp Are You In?

Since you're reading this book (and I sincerely appreciate that you are), you at least fall into the Consumer camp. The question is whether you are reaching your potential when it comes to your own leadership development. Here are some questions to challenge your introspection on the subject:

- Have you prioritized your consumption of leadership content as a critical factor in determining your influence?
- In what ways could you better translate the lessons you are personally learning and transmit them to your sphere of influence?
- How are you verifying that those you lead are passing on your input to their subordinates?

- If leader development is really a priority for you and your team, how are you checking to ensure your followers are developing the right habits to facilitate growth in the right areas?
- Is leadership stagnation a "fireable offense" in your organization? If not, how are you keeping your growing leaders from being dragged down by the unmotivated?

How Effective is Your Leadership Narrative?

Pop quiz:

- What methods are best for inspiring the team after failure?
- How long are you willing to wait for information after an initial report?
- How long should a leader wait before jumping in to resolve internal team conflict?
- What kind of failure would cause you to relieve a subordinate?
- When is micromanagement appropriate?

And one more question: How did you meet your spouse?

The last question should be much easier to answer. Why is that? It's not like the other questions aren't important. They're just a bit nebulous, subjective, and abstract ... and you probably don't think about them very often.

The story of meeting your spouse, however, is clear, memorable, and specific. You lived the experience with anticipation and emotional permanency, recounting the story many times since. You know how to tell that story, complete with suspense and inflection to make it enjoyable. It's a familiar narrative.

What I want to assert now is that the best leaders are as familiar with their leadership narrative, their perspective on the fundamental components of leadership, as they are with the story of meeting their spouse.

What is a Leadership Narrative?

A leadership narrative is the tangible representation of your leadership DNA. It originates from your worldview, biases, experiences, and beliefs, and is literally the combination of thoughts, words, examples, stories, assertions, and guidance that you communicate as a leader.

What's so Important About the Leadership Narrative?

Great leadership does not happen by accident, and neither does a coherent leadership narrative. A leader with a solidified leadership perspective ponders the varying facets of the environment in which she leads. This leader routinely engages in topics of leadership, ethics, organizational development, training, and so on.

In having these regular interactions, she brings hazy beliefs and scattered thoughts into focus, coalescing them into guidance that is vetted and has intellectual and emotional legitimacy. This effort serves as a rehearsal for future decisions she will make and challenges she will face.

The leader with a formed leadership narrative will face fewer surprises than the person who has resisted this form of personal growth. She will have rational responses to abstract situations and emotional stability when others don't. When the leader with no engaged passion for leadership is still grappling with the dynamics of a problem, the leader with narrative will already be solving it.

How to Develop Your Leadership Narrative?

I mentioned above that the best leaders talk regularly about leadership. They weave it into daily interactions, which give them opportunity to hear opposing perspectives, test theories, and hone their own arguments. Discussion, however, is only part of a holistic approach to developing a leadership narrative, which looks like this: **Consumption – Distillation – Reflection – Refinement – Transmission**

"You are today where your thoughts have brought you;
you will be tomorrow where your thoughts take you."
~ James Allen

The process begins with **consumption**. The leader with a narrative to develop actively seeks out and consumes high-quality professional content. Books, professional journals, online magazines, blogs, conferences, and many other sources make up the leader's consumption menu. Consumption of professional content is such a pivotally decisive step to great leadership that I'm convinced no success can be found without it.

The leader then **distills** (or filters) the most relevant of that content to identify what will become part of his leadership narrative. If reading a book is consumption, distillation is underlining a passage that resonates. Mentors and leader development programs play an important role here by helping junior leaders extract appropriate insight from professional sources.

Reflection is the step a leader takes in shaping the distilled content into personalized insight. For example, after underlining a book passage, the reflection step is writing in the margins to capture how the text is specifically relevant and applicable. Reflection is intellectually challenging. Anyone can pick out a brilliant quote, but the great leader is able to convert that insight into lessons that resonate in her own leadership environment. Leaders can also draw insight from experience, provided that they are open to learning from that experience.

Refinement is the core of developing a narrative, and the step in which leaders often fail to fully engage. In refinement, leaders consolidate the insight they gained from professional content and experience then continually expose it to the real world. They discuss their thoughts on leadership with their network of peers and mentors, hearing new perspectives and defending beliefs. They say things like, "Hey, I read the other day that … What do you think?" or "A mentor recommended I deal with a situation like so, how would you do it?"

Writing and publishing are also excellent ways to refine the leadership narrative. Putting words to paper consolidates beliefs and requires specificity that casual conversation does not. As Michael Hyatt says, *"Thoughts disentangle themselves over the lips and through fingertips."*

Transmission. A leadership narrative is purely academic unless the leader transmits it to his sphere of influence. If the preceding steps give the leader an arsenal of insight to apply across the organization, transmission is the deployment of that insight at the right time and place, and to the right people. Transmission is not just regurgitation. It is how a leader uses her particular skills to solve unique problems. Transmission is the art of leadership.

Become the Leader You Were Meant to Be

New insight does not simply appear. It is formed from the consumption of professional content, growth brought on by experience, and the refinement that everyday discussion brings. Great leaders navigate this process intentionally, honing their leadership narrative so that they are ready when problems arise. The leadership narrative is an intimate familiarity with the type of leader one seeks to be, a familiarity that allows the leader to employ his talent with the same coherence, comfort, and excitement that he tells the story of meeting his spouse.

Maybe now is the time for you to energize your leadership narrative by evaluating how your leadership skills develop. Challenge the efficacy of what content you consume, engage your network to refine your thoughts, and shape your message to reflect a coherent narrative. In doing so, you will prime yourself for the quality of leadership you will one day have to exhibit.

This Mindset Shift Changes Everything

What I love about leadership is that it is highly individualized. We may strive to display commonly held principles for successful leadership—lead by example, mentor junior leaders, exhibit poise during stress—but the way we describe our leadership styles, the personality traits we employ, the perspectives we adopt, the anecdotes we use are all different, shaped by unique experiences and beliefs. This individualization creates an endless reservoir of leadership insight from which to learn and draw out of others.

A mentor of mine virtually introduced me to a successful Air Force Colonel living in the city I was traveling to. We linked up for a beer and not only did the conversation turn to leadership, but he delivered a dose of wisdom so fundamental that it instantly related to everything I do as a leader and revamped my approach to bringing out the best in organizations.

Lose Control

This Air Force Colonel said that **too many people impose their authority on the organization and call it leadership.** Because their success is riding on the team's performance, leaders seek increasing amounts of control over the organization's activities. They have a habit of trying to make their people execute exactly how they would do it, which dismisses subordinate growth and fails to leverage the talent that individuals could contribute to resolving the problem.

He said that leaders could easily unlock the talent of their organizations by shifting their mindset from one of *control* to one of *growth*.

Look at the transformation that occurs when a leader's mindset shifts from *"My job is at stake; I must direct this team to excellence"* to *"My role is to draw out excellence by providing opportunities to perform."* The latter perspective espouses the belief that if given the opportunity (and sometimes the inspiration), followers will reach a higher level of excellence through growth than the leader could induce by telling them how to get the mission done.

In this approach, mission accomplishment is simply a byproduct of the team's growth, not a result brought about by the force of the leader's will. It's another aspect of legendary UCLA coach John Wooden's philosophy : "The best way to build a winning team is to elevate each player's level of talent." When they each grow into better players, the team's talent grows exponentially.

Follower-Centric Leadership

This mindset shift radically transforms the follower experience. In your career, you've probably seen how much more inspiring it is to follow a leader who is more concerned about subordinate growth than he is about his own reputation. Those leaders stand out. They care about their people and think of them first. Consequently, those leaders tap into their organizations' full potential and draw talent out of the next generation of leaders. This is the essence of selfless service.

How can we create this mindset? Instead of worrying about sustaining their own position by preventing failure in the face of a challenging situation, leaders could start by exploring how to maximize their followers' development.

Instead of asking, *"How do I get them to do it my way?"*, ask questions like:

- What methods can I use to draw out the creative power of this team?
- What distractions can I eliminate so the team can focus on the mission?
- How can I shape this event to maximize the strengths of the team?

- What creative scenarios can I inject that will challenge the team members and bring them together?
- What conditions will make the experience more emotionally permanent?
- How can I help my followers draw the best lessons from this event?
- What can I let my followers discover on their own instead of just telling them?

Asking these questions requires you to give up a little control, and that's ok. **When you give them the opportunity, you will see people rise to the occasion.** Set conditions for them to contribute their best effort and you might just discover that the need to maintain control was never even necessary.

Leadership from the Heart

There's one more point to share about the counsel I received from the seasoned leader. He wasn't preaching theory. His advice was the core of the leadership philosophy he had used through multiple commands. He truly cared about developing those around him, which was plainly evident by the way he invested in my own growth after only just meeting.

And that's the way leadership has to be … from the heart, personal. You can't care about yourself more than you care about developing those you lead.

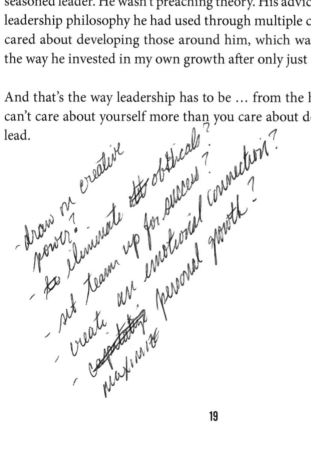

Putting Ego in Its Place

"Never let your ego get so close to your position,
so that when your position goes, your ego goes with it."
~ General Colin Powell

It's easy to assume a position of leadership or take the guidon of command, and think that we were made for the job—that the organization and its people need us there—or that we were ordained to lead.

The responsibility and the recognition of being a leader make it natural to align our self-worth with our job. It can become who we are, our identity. Similarly, many of us display attitudes/emotions that fluctuate with how we think we are *performing* in our jobs (i.e., a bad day at work means a bad day at home).

General Colin Powell warns against letting the job overcome who we are, because one day the titles and responsibility will drift away, then what are we left with?

We should keep in mind a few key characteristics about leading in the military:

- The unit you are leading is not yours; it's the government's.
- The government didn't create the job for you; it exists for the Nation's people.
- The unit and its members will continue to excel even after you leave.

It's prudent to find a way to display passion for the work while appropriately divorcing emotional stability and self-worth. We can't take the work's esteem with us when we go. We can only focus on making a positive impact that outlasts our tenure.

The other valuable lesson to find in General Powell's statement is how ego should relate to future jobs and career goals we seek.

A few years ago I had the opportunity to compete for a highly-competitive position on a team that holds unmatched regard in the military. It was the kind of job that, if chosen, would give me instant credibility and esteem in my professional community.

As you might imagine, this opportunity draws the most motivated and talented Soldiers from across the military. Unfortunately for most, the opportunity is also highly and dispassionately selective. Incredibly capable Soldiers prepare for years, only to find out they don't meet the narrow bandwidth of acceptable talent and are sent home, which is what happened to me.

During the process, however, I saw peers become obsessed with being selected, making it the ultimate validation of their military career—the definitive stamp of individual self-worth and achievement. They clearly aligned their egos with the position, and many took an emotional hit when they weren't accepted.

Powell's advice is clear wisdom for those with competitive career goals. It's wise to remain stoic about the outcome, particularly if the goal is highly-selective. Becoming psychologically tied to a career goal can easily cause one to:

- Miss other opportunities during the process
- Make poor decisions because of the emotional investment and fear of failure
- Fail to see the positive aspects of the resulting situation
- Set a poor example for peers and subordinates who are striving to achieve their own goals
- Place an emotional toll on peers and family who will provide support in any outcome

Bottom Line

No organization, job title, or status can invalidate the commitment, talent, and influence one achieves during an entire career. Separate who you are from what you do and be selective about where you place your self-worth.

separate who you are from what you do.

Prevent Power from Corrupting Your Leadership

We are all familiar with the warning that "power corrupts." And if you're like me, when you hear the phrase, the first type of corrupted power you think of is greed. The ruthless Gordon Gekko from *Wall Street* comes to mind. If you shift the phrase to the military frame of reference, you might think of generals breaking joint ethics regulations on TDY travel and contracting, or perhaps the senior leader with the moral lapse.

The commonality among these individuals is a feeling of invincibility that either distorts judgment or severs behavior from prudent thought. When power is involved, we are all at risk.

The Subtle Shift

Something happened when I took command for the first time years ago. When I woke up that morning I had no authority, no official leadership position, and little influence. But by 1100, I had more authority than I'd ever had before ... *and* it was reinforced by the Uniform Code of Military Justice! Sure, I had a boss, but I also had power to run things the way I wanted to.

Most of us, however, wouldn't immediately take this power to the extreme and start upending the organization. We have some humility, some perspective, and some deference to our bosses that keeps us in check. The problem isn't that we would take the mantle of leadership and declare our omnipotence as leaders. The problem is that over time, **our increasing** comfort with power *nudges us towards* feelings of omnipotence and unless restrained, could lead to disaster.

"WW__D?"

In more recent years I had the experience that, through rotational attrition, I became the senior member of a fairly autonomous staff team. On the team, I had routinely sought guidance from the more experienced members, which informed my judgment and tempered my actions. When facing problems, I asked myself, *"What would LTC ___ do in this situation?"*

Similar to the first day in command, I took over this team and immediately realized it was *my* opinion that mattered most (and first) in the course of our duties. The heads were turned to me. So I did what anyone would do … I started slinging out answers.

What I didn't remember to do was continue asking, *"What would ___ do?"*

One day I was checking my work against a mentor's example; the next I was making decisions based entirely on my own abilities. And that's where the risk is. **Transitioning from groupie to rock star happens all the time in the military—the key is not to lose perspective when it does.** Start thinking you're God's gift to the organization and you stop challenging the strength of your leadership. You stop asking *"What if I'm wrong?"*, which is a powerful question for leaders to habitually ask.

Start with Velcro

As your rock star moment comes up, here are some ideas to prevent power from distorting your influence:

- **Remember that your rank is held on by Velcro.** A boss of mine once promoted a Colonel to Brigadier General with the warning that it takes a lifetime to earn the rank but only a second to rip it off. There's a lesson about keeping yourself out of trouble, but also one about humility.
- **Keep asking, *"WW_D?"*** It helps to keep in mind the example of a trusted mentor or a professional whose performance you

respect. Don't try to be someone else, but you can compare your thoughts against their example to refine and improve your leadership.

- **Clearly define problems before dishing out answers.** If you have the decision authority, you probably have some control over the decision window. Avoid responding to every problem with your first instinct, especially in the beginning of your tenure. Take a moment (or a day) to clarify what is being asked, what the relevant factors are, who the key players are, what resources the problem will require, and what effects you want to achieve for your team. Then start issuing guidance. You will see two important effects: 1) You will increase the quality of your decisions, and 2) You will teach your team the level of analysis you expect from them before presenting future problems.

- **Create a conduit of accountability.** As you gain authority (and usually autonomy along with it), find someone you trust and give them license to provide honest feedback. You could choose your senior enlisted advisor, your spouse, or a peer leader. Run your challenges and decisions by this person for a sanity check. As a side note, some people think forming this type of relationship with peer leaders (i.e., people you are evaluated against) is professionally risky. I disagree. The endstate of such lateral mentorship is ultimately better leadership for the Soldiers and stronger bonds between adjacent unit leaders. Those effects far outweigh concerns about career progression. (Read more about this in "How to Survive a Shrinking Army.")

- **Ask input from those you lead.** Yes, it's ok to ask how you are doing as a leader. Are you communicating your message effectively? Are you attending to the critical needs of your followers? Do you micromanage your staff or perhaps give too little guidance? Do intermediate leaders dilute your vision for the organization before it gets to the troops? We all think we're hitting home runs until we open our eyes and see that the balls are barely clearing the infield. Ask the lowest level in your organization how things are going and you'll gain invaluable perspective.

- **Maintain a habit of growth.** It's impossible to think you have all the answers if you have a habit of learning. Put another way, if you stop learning, it's easy to think that you have all the answers (talent) you need to succeed. Acquiring new knowledge keeps you intellectually humble, which is a priceless trait for leaders to possess. Stay on the growth journey with books, videos, podcasts, articles, blogs, and conversations that elevate.

Getting Your Mental Map Realigned

In his book *Deep Survival*, author Laurence Gonzales describes how the brain assembles a "mental map" of the world based on spatial orientation, experience, emotion, cognition, and every other facet of who we are. This mental map is our unique perspective of the world. It's our comfort zone. It's what we rest on; it's where we feel safe.

But there's a problem in that our mental map doesn't always align with "the real map," i.e., the real world.

Gonzales relates numerous accounts in which people found themselves in survival situations and continued to cling to their old reality: the one where they were still sitting safely in a plane at 30,000 feet or the one where a bear hadn't just wrecked their campsite leaving them stranded. The people who died are the ones who failed to update their mental maps to their new situations.

The essential point is that sometimes there is a fate lying just around the corner that we have never, EVER considered, but will have to react to.

Sadr City

In 2008, such a "new fate" arrived in Sadr City, Iraq. By March, the urban enclave of two million people in northeastern Baghdad had quieted down to the point that just two companies of Stryker Infantry were needed to contain it. We had regular meetings with local leaders and enemy attacks were very low. Some might say that we had reached "steady-state operations," and a routine of stability. We were in a comfort zone.

But as the saying goes, the enemy gets a vote, and Muqtada al-Sadr's vote came at the end of March, when he unleashed an hourly barrage of rocket, mortar, IED, RPG, and gunfire attacks on the Baghdad Green Zone and units in the area. In a matter of hours, the tactical situation in Sadr City shifted from low- to high-intensity, with engagements akin to the *Black Hawk Down* depiction of Mogadishu in 1993. The digital map erupted red icons all over the city as our units tried to get a handle on the emerging situation. The enemy had achieved surprise and units were sustaining casualties.

Sadr City is a perfect example of a situation that requires leaders to reframe their mental maps to the new reality. Holding on to the prior trend of stability was pointless and risky. We needed a new plan, and fast.

The command deployed additional assets from surrounding areas and blocked the routes in and out of the city, then platoons fought their way north to reclaim a key road. Where two companies once occupied, 14 companies now stood.

The resulting month-long fight ultimately reduced the Sadr militia's combat power and a new 2.4 km wall across the city prevented them from affecting key coalition bases. From the Soldiers on the street to the Commanding General, the dramatic change in the tactical landscape demanded mental agility, measured emotional response, and poised leadership.

Bottom Line

The lesson is that leaders must be open-minded enough to sense a changing environment, willing to discard what is comfortable and accept the new reality, and then be decisive in the *new environment,* not the old.

Leaders also need to accept that unseen realities exist and have momentum along tracks that will ultimately intersect with and affect the organization. Muqtada al-Sadr had likely been planning the March 2008 offensive for months. Intelligence efforts, of course, seek to discover these initiatives, but leaders must live in a state of open-ended readiness to adjust and lead their organizations through change.

Tragedy and Readiness — Fort Hood's Lesson

The April 2014 shooting at Fort Hood, TX was a sad, unnecessary tragedy that no community should have to live through. And until the fabric of our society grows past this trend in violence, we will have to continue to prepare for such events. When these tragedies do occur, how the involved leaders respond can determine how damaging the events become, as well as how the public reacts to them.

Unpredictability will be a hallmark it seems, as will national media attention. This means that the small-town sheriff, or the unknown hospital supervisor, or the base's commanding general could progress from a position of "business as usual" to "nationally-televised responsibility" in a matter of hours.

Put another way: The most challenging event in a leader's life could be just around the corner.

Even though Fort Hood's commanding general was no stranger to summoning peak performance at critical moments, he didn't start April 2, 2014 thinking he'd be mitigating a terrible crisis with an audience of millions. What does this example show?

Leaders must live in the mindset that their talents will be put to the test in some unimaginable, untested way, caused by an event that is alarmingly unpredictable. Leaders will have to show staunchness in seeing the tragedy through, while at the same time empathizing and consoling members of their organization. They'll have to find a surge of energy at the end of an already-long day, and then continue that pace for weeks. This means they will have had to live a life of readiness, having developed both the talents and the physical/mental capacity to endure the test.

what defines success? then, there are multiple stakeholders - do they align?

"The Energy Comes from You"

We had just departed the aircraft at 500 feet, landed, then assembled at the edge of the drop zone to start a multi-day training evaluation of our skills as an Infantry platoon. It was Fort Bragg, North Carolina in August, so of course the weather was blazing hot and stiflingly humid. This was the first true test of my leadership skills and I was about to receive the best piece of advice of my career.

The platoon was spread out across the woodline and ready to begin the patrol to locate and destroy enemy in the area. I knelt down to verify our map position and give the order to begin the patrol when I felt an overwhelming presence over my right shoulder.

My battalion commander, a Lieutenant Colonel with 18 more years of experience than I had and commander of our 750-man unit, had quietly walked up behind me and was watching my every action. When he knelt down next to me, I expected criticism, "What are you waiting for, Lieutenant?"

Instead, he locked eyes with me, leaned in, and said: *"Remember … the energy comes from you."*

The lesson immediately clicked with me. This is what he was saying:

- **You are in charge.** There should be no doubt in your mind—or anyone else's—about who is leading this patrol.
- **You set the tone.** How you react to each situation will determine how the Soldiers will react. If you bark frenzied instructions, your

subordinate leaders will transmit that tension to the Soldiers. But if you remain calm in execution, you'll infuse confidence in the formation.

- **You provide the organizational momentum.** This is about to be a very long exercise with multiple challenging engagements. Fatigue will bring the platoon to a halt unless you motivate the team and set an example of discipline.
- **You are responsible.** If the platoon fails, you get the blame; if it succeeds, your Soldiers get the credit.

Then, as if to immediately prove the point, he said, *"Now, get after it!"*

An Open Letter to Cadets

Whether graduation is weeks or years away, the countdown that started at 1,460 days will eventually come to an end. Imagine it for a moment. You and your anxious cohort are seated for the ceremony. Proud parents are watching from the stands. The National Anthem is cued. Commencement speakers are on the stage. It's your last day in a cadet uniform.

As you prepare for that moment, I invite you to keep close at heart the advice of Major C.A. Bach in a farewell address to the Student Officers at Fort Sheridan, c. 1919:

> *"These commissions will not make you leaders,*
> *they will merely make you officers."*

Whether you find yourself in a sterile research lab, in a cockpit at 40,000 feet, or in front of a formation of Infantry troops, every one of you will step into an environment that requires leadership. Leadership is everywhere people are. It is the element that converts the potential energy of our organizations into mission accomplishment. Without quality leadership, we fail.

Unfortunately, while in school some cadets will pursue a myriad of other college interests while assuming that the commissioning ceremony will magically bestow upon them the leadership talent required for success. In reality, leadership is so much more than wearing gold bars and issuing orders. It develops over a long journey of rigorous study, reflection, and hard-fought experience.

And that growth does not happen passively, as no one drifts into leadership excellence. If you want to be a capable leader on your first day as an officer, leadership must be a deliberate part of your cadet experience – a daily personal pursuit and not simply an academic class to be passed and forgotten. Find ten minutes a day to do something—anything—that relates to leadership or improves your future ability to exert positive influence on those you will lead. Books and articles are great; jotting notes and penning your own thoughts are even better.

Have at least one conversation per day that surpasses the mundane and includes words like: integrity, honor, influence, loyalty, discipline, character, respect, initiative, fairness, responsibility, clarity, excellence, growth, reward, failure, example, emotion, passion, ethics, perseverance, trust, expectation, duty, vision, effectiveness, inspiration, and humility.

Why? Because this is the language of leaders, and it's tough to use these words in conversation without learning something meaningful.

Finally, get your leadership radar up. By that, I mean you should be open to discerning and internalizing leadership lessons that present themselves throughout your day. Actively note the behavior of others you wish to model, and even those you don't. This trait not only fills your kit bag with useful knowledge you will rely on later, it will train you to be an intuitive leader in years to come.

Great leadership talent is tough to acquire, harder to implement, and always fleeting. As such, shape your cadet experience today so you will be prepared for the challenges that await tomorrow. And heed the insight of the 19th Century English theologian, H.P. Liddon, who said:

"What we do on some great occasion will depend on what we are; and what we are will be the result of previous years of self-discipline."

Beyond Lieutenant Time

In his 2014 Modern War Institute article, Army First Lieutenant Scott Ginther related 20 lessons from his path from West Point Cadet to Platoon Leader in Afghanistan.

Much credit goes to 1LT Ginther for clearly learning the right lessons as a young leader, and for taking the time to capture and share them with the force. I offer the following thoughts as an addendum to his insights, and intend them to show how the leadership environment changes in the transition from Lieutenant to Commander and Field Grade officer.

You're Still Not a Trigger-puller

As a Company Commander and Field Grade officer, you begin to transition away from direct leadership and more towards system management. You emplace a fitness plan in your company; you create a Welcome/In-processing procedure for the battalion; you oversee the staff during mission planning. These responsibilities aren't glamorous, but they keep the unit and Soldiers moving forward safely and effectively. But don't forget, you will still have to excel individually when Soldiers look to you personally for an example (physical fitness events, unit history, etc).

"Being" a Leader Is No Longer Enough

When you become a Captain, then certainly as a Major, the Army expects that you have learned and grown enough to start **building leaders** instead of just leading followers. This means you'll have to solidify the type of leader you want to be and establish a plan for how you'll develop your Soldiers and officers. You should capture thoughts and lessons, and then share them with your expanding network. You will be investing in the future of the Army, so make the effort to build the type of leader you want to work for.

Your Performance Impacts Families

Becoming a commander and a field grade officer means that your decisions and the quality of your leadership start to impact families. How you treat your Soldiers will have ripple effects in their personal lives. The care you put into the Family Readiness Group will have a tangible effect on unit morale and individual commitment to the team. If you neglect the family component of command, not only will you suffer as a leader, but more importantly you'll likely prevent good Soldiers from reenlisting.

The Consequences of Your Actions Increase Exponentially

It's not that you can't do a lot of damage by being a bad platoon leader ... you can. But the further you progress in your career, your "cog in the wheel" will become bigger and bigger. And the consequences of your failure become catastrophic to mission and Soldiers. It's the effect of the systems environment you'll be in.

Example: young Soldier arrives to your company from another installation. You've haven't emplaced a system for the leaders under your command to properly execute reception and integration. And with the fast-paced environment, the Soldier goes right to work; so, no one knows he has a history of misconduct. He spends his first weekend night exploring the new bars and kills himself while driving back. It may not be your fault—he was under the influence of alcohol and crashed—but a thorough integration and counseling plan would have flagged your leaders to mitigate areas of risk and might have saved him.

Rehearsals Can Save an Operation

A well-rehearsed operation can make up for poor planning, but even a great plan will likely fail without rehearsals. You've got to recognize the critical and vulnerable points of an operation and rehearse them to perfection. Tactically, those points will likely be: moving out of the assembly area; when forces join, move to support each other, or deploy to the objective; and at the point of employment for numerous weapon systems. Rehearsals will teach the organization synchronization, tactical patience, and adjacent coordination. In garrison, critical points will include any event that: involves families, begins after a 4-day weekend, or includes your senior rater.

Maximize Adjacent Power

As a company commander you won't have a staff. Your platoon leaders will be doing what they do, and oftentimes "you're it" when it comes to creative genius. Engage your fellow commanders often and share your ideas. This not only increases your collective knowledge and improves the unit as a whole, but it gives you a sanity check on your thoughts and your interpretation of your boss's intent.

Be a Team Player

Heads-up! Your boss will judge you based on whether or not you are a team player. Nothing in the military is about the individual and, when the chips are down, your commander will want subordinate leaders who will support each other, not try to outshine one another. Share your products, ideas, tools, and lessons learned from failure.

Lose the Attitude

There's nothing more frustrating than a talented subordinate who has the attitude that the unit owes him something. It's almost a rite of passage for Lieutenants and junior Captains to go through the cynical phase. My advice: Go through it fast. You'll have to prove yourself in your new unit following the Career Course and you don't want people to think you're entitled or holier-than-thou. As the saying goes, "It ain't what ya done, it's what ya done lately."

Microsoft Is Not a "Leadership Tool," But You'd Better Know How to Use It

True, jumping right to PowerPoint is rarely a good way to start solving a problem, but name a system the military uses more than Microsoft. If it's not our most powerful weapon system, it's certainly our most prolific. Knowing your digital way around is important because it increases your efficiency (which frees you to do other tasks), and it increases your ability to communicate your message. Believe me, staff Captain, if you don't show yourself adept at Microsoft Office, your Type-A Operations Officer will take over the keyboard and do it himself (and you don't want that).

What Made You Successful As a Cadet Can Make You Successful As a Field Grade ... IF You Keep Up the Habits

Too many officers slack on fitness and professional development because they think they've "arrived" and have "been there." The fact is, the good leaders never "get there." Your successful peers will be the ones who take the positive traits learned as cadets (discipline, pursuit of excellence, and reading, among others) and continue to apply them to Army life.

The Homework Shouldn't Stop

The Army divides its model of leader development into three domains: Individual, Organizational (unit experience), and Institutional (professional schooling). Many officers think that they only need to study while attending the Career Course or the Command and General Staff College, and that their "experience" trumps any academic development the Army could give them. Such an attitude is foolish. There is no reason you can't assign your platoon leaders and NCOs periodic doctrinal or historical reading, which will provide enlightened perspectives from which to view real-world experiences. We all think we are working as hard as we can, but truth is that there's probably more we could be doing to improve.

You May Not Be the Best Captain/Major Ever ... But You Can Certainly Separate Yourself From the Pack

As a Lieutenant, it's true that you probably feel like part of the herd, just marching along trying not to get fired. Transitioning through company command, however, is your first opportunity to distinguish yourself with your performance. Your peers will find civilian jobs and your year group will shrink. Your first big gate will be your company command evaluation, which will formally stamp you as Average or Above Center Mass, and hopefully start the trend of documented excellence. You'll start to be senior-rated by Colonels with big reputations and you will pick up mentors who will campaign for your career and pull you into jobs in later years.

All this is important, because if you want to command a battalion one day, you'll need to have the following: a long trend of above-average performance, the right jobs to prepare you, and a circle of mentors to guide you. None of this happens by accident, so be intentional about your performance and your career.

BZ Doesn't Matter

If you hang your hat on making Major below-the-zone, your ego is in for an ugly awakening. BZ doesn't matter, and it's not an accurate discriminator of talent. If anything, it's a hindrance because you lose time to develop yourself with broadening jobs at higher echelons.

Get a Master's Degree

A significant majority of those selected to command battalions hold masters degrees. Higher education shows the Army that you are committed to learning and aren't afraid to keep working hard. Make sure you get it before your key position as a Major or you aren't likely to do it.

The Parent as Leader

Finally, 1LT Ginther did a great job in pointing out that his parents taught him to be a better leader. One fascinating aspect of leaving your Lieutenant years is that you will likely also become a parent, which will in turn impact you as a leader. Many leaders under-appreciate or don't anticipate the effect that parenthood will have on them (not the least of which is sleep deprivation worse than Ranger School).

Personally, I gained a newfound sense of empathy for military families as a group, and specifically for the families of those I was leading. (I now know how sickening it is to not see my children for days because of late office nights. So, I've changed the way I lead so that subordinates don't have to experience that, if possible.) Building a family of my own has also taught me that "family resilience" is relative, so I don't assume that a Soldier's difficulty at home is something he should automatically be able to handle. Being an Army parent is hard, so give them the benefit of the doubt and help them through it.

These lessons are just a sampling of the countless insights that junior officers will discover if they care about developing as leaders and professionals. If you've learned a lesson along the way, there's a good chance that one of your subordinates could benefit from hearing about it, so don't forget to teach what you know.

"You Are Being Watched" — A Lesson in Example

Years ago, as I approached my commissioning as a Second Lieutenant, a mentor was describing Army life to me and said something memorable about example. He pointed out,

> "You will pass probably a hundred Soldiers throughout each day … and you're gonna have to salute each one of them … and it will start to feel routine and unimportant, almost an annoyance. But don't get sloppy and don't take it for granted. You won't remember each one of those Soldiers, but they will remember you. You may be the only officer a Soldier sees that day … the only salute he sees in return. So execute each interaction as if it were the most important of the day."

There is clearly the "professional bearing and appearance" side of my mentor's lesson, the idea that a leader, whether she likes it or not, is on a perpetual stage. Every moment is an opportunity to represent the organization's values and telegraph desirable performance standards. Appearance matters. Doing correct push-ups matters. Training to standard matters. And suffering hardship with the team matters.

> *"Be an example to your men, in your duty and*
> *in private life. Never spare yourself*
> *and let your troops see that you don't in your*
> *endurance of fatigue and privation."*
> ~ German Field Marshal Erwin Rommel

"You are always on parade."
~ General George S. Patton, Jr.

The other aspect is that leaders influence followers in ways that are less-direct and more personal. Just as you have chosen what talents you like about your leaders, your followers get to choose what traits they will model after you. Each person views your leadership from a different perspective and a different set of needs. Some are looking for perseverance during busy times. Others are disgruntled and need the passion reignited. Some need a good lesson in humility. Still others will bend their parenting behavior to model your character traits.

Bottom Line

You don't get to decide which lessons people take from your example or when they decide to learn from your behavior. You're always "on" and you will likely never discover the true impact of your leadership. This is both the burden and the blessing of leadership … make it count.

Marshall on the Combat Leader

You'll need to read this General George C. Marshall quote several times to absorb all the lessons hidden within it. He was speaking to officer candidates in September of 1941:

> When you are commanding, leading [soldiers] under conditions where physical exhaustion and privations must be ignored, where the lives of [soldiers] may be sacrificed, then, the efficiency of your leadership will depend only to a minor degree on your tactical ability. It will primarily be determined by your character, your reputation, not much for courage—which will be accepted as a matter of course—but by the previous reputation you have established for fairness, for that high-minded patriotic purpose, that quality of unswerving determination to carry through any military task assigned to you.

[handwritten margin note: crisis leadership is about the relationship you establish ahead of time]

What should you take away from Marshall's advice?

- The "starting line" for leadership in combat is that one must accept, ignore, and discard the physical hardship that accompanies it. Exhaustion is the innate price of participation. Thus, leaders should maintain a physical fitness level that allows them to fulfill their command duties despite fatigue.
- Tactical ability in combat is not as important as character. This is a tough concept to grasp, but it helps to ask, "Which is more dangerous in combat, a lack of tactical ability or a lack of character?" Marshall seems to indicate that inexperienced commanders can

still succeed in combat by making common sense, informed decisions, and that an organization can absorb a leader's lack of tactical ability. However, a commander lacking character will have more destructive and permanent effects on an organization.

- Courage is the default for a combat leader. Similar to endurance under privation, Marshall says that courage in combat is a given, and expected by Soldiers. Is this concept in line with our view of courage in combat today?
- What does create success for a commander in combat? Marshall says plainly that character is decisive above all else. Character accompanied with perseverance under any conditions, fairness in decision making, and a clear attitude of service to the Nation.

Five Must-Have Conversations for Military Leaders

I learned an important lesson on the first day of my new command in a headquarters company in 2007. I had already commanded a rifle company and thought that I had pretty much honed the skills needed to succeed again. (Maybe I was giving myself too much credit?) The change of command ceremony concluded and I walked into my new office to find my First Sergeant waiting. He said, *"Sir, do you have a few minutes?"* *"Of course,"* I replied.

What followed was one of the most enabling and professionally developing exchanges I've had in my entire career. Yes, this First Sergeant is exceptionally talented and would teach me more about leadership than any other NCO I've worked with, but the conversation was powerful because he and I synchronized how we would lead the company together. We discussed everything from combat to family readiness to weight control. We spent hours together that day and set the tone for success because we got aligned from day one.

Today, I think back on that experience and realize that I would've been a fool NOT to have had that conversation, and that there are actually a few more areas in the military leader's life where a frank and honest conversation is necessary to enable success.

Your Boss

Whether due to personality traits, proximity, or just busy schedules, some people don't spend much time with their boss. You don't want to be in that situation. You need to lock-in time with your rater and senior rater to make sure you're aligned with their efforts and expectations. You need to ask what success in your job looks like and how you can better enable your higher command's priorities. Ask about their leadership style, personality traits, and how much information they need to feel satisfied that you're getting the job done. Then, follow up with regular appointments (not always a formal counseling session) to ensure you're still on track.

Your Senior Enlisted Leader

As I mentioned above, the conversation with my First Sergeant at the outset of our command journey together was necessary to set conditions for success. If you're an officer, there is no more important team member than your senior enlisted leader. He has a wealth of experience and has probably already walked every road you'll encounter during your tenure. He will be the action arm of your leadership, so it's crucial that you get aligned early and challenge each other's opinions to ensure you're always on the same page.

Your Assignment Officer

In this book, you will see that I'm a fan of engaging your Human Resources Command Assignment Officer. You need to map the major steps on your career path and confirm that your timeline matches your expectations. You also need to ask her where you stand in relation to your peers and if your file supports your long-term goals.

Your Spouse

Your spouse is the most influential person in your military career. If he/she doesn't have a full understanding of what it means to serve in the military or how long you plan to serve, then you're on a potentially disastrous road. Your spouse needs to be part of your regular professional engagement plan, if for no other reason than to give him/her a sense of what you're experiencing in your career.

Husbands/wives of service members have a unique set of sacrifices to make. They will be more prepared to face those challenges if they understand what each phase of the career will bring and are involved in making decisions about the future.

Yourself

> *"No man is fit to command another who cannot command himself."*
> ~ William Penn

Finally, before you expend effort aligning with the people around you, you must solidify who you are in each of your roles as service member, leader, spouse, parent, etc. You have to spend reflective time figuring out your beliefs on the myriad of major engagement areas that will arise in your career. How will you develop your people? How will you handle misconduct? How late are you willing to stay at work? Do you want to serve through retirement?

It's unreasonable to ask the people around you to share your journey if you're not sure where you're going. It's the most important conversation you'll have.

Three Traits That Will Get You Fired

When was the last time you saw a military peer get fired from a position? Doesn't happen too often, right? In the civilian world, the last several years have been characterized by high unemployment and a difficult job market, even for new college graduates. In contrast, the military is intentionally difficult to enter, but also hard to be removed from. Why is that?

Several reasons come into play:

- The military invests a lot of time and resources in developing specialized skills.
- The nature of service is honorable and we give the service member much credit for volunteering to serve.
- Service members are not easily replaced.
- The military asks a lot of its service members, so it gives a lot of leeway for marginal behavior.
- Service members typically move every 2–3 years, so supervisors can "wait out" bad performance and pass it down the line.

As a leader, you have mediocre performers on your team, the ones who fulfill their duty and not much more. They keep the organization running by learning just enough to progress in the military's "up or out" system. They're not destructive, they're just there.

But how do you identify the bad apples, the ones who will have a corrosive or even dangerous effect on your unit or another unit down the road? What subordinate traits are unacceptable and worthy of dismissal?

Consider these three traits:

- **Lack of integrity.** Integrity is a clear line in the sand, especially as rank increases. Integrity is so common among our community that we often assume it is a default trait for all service members and fail to assess or teach it enough. Leaders must aggressively investigate any hint of integrity violations, as they are not problems that will fix themselves.
- **Inability to work with others.** The military mission rests completely on teamwork. Whether deployed or in garrison, a subordinate who cannot interact with others is a threat to the unit's cohesion. Every service member must be able to engage, converse, and share responsibility with those around him. Failing to do so erodes the most important characteristic of capable teams: trust.
- **Resistance to growth.** A subordinate with no willingness to develop is without question useless. They need to grow as technical experts of their skill, and they need to grow as leaders. Leaders should publicize personal development as a "No-Fail" task and take active steps to evaluate subordinates on their relative growth.

How to Survive a Shrinking Army ~~Company~~

In 2014, while discussing the separation boards and low promotion rates in light of a downsizing Army, a fellow officer commented, "These trends are going to create a cutthroat Army. Everyone is going to watch their backs and protect themselves to make sure they get promoted. I'm not looking forward to serving in that environment."

With all due respect to his perspective and opinion, that's the wrong way to approach the coming years in our Army. And specifically, that's the wrong attitude to have if you want to get promoted and continue to lead Soldiers. Here's why:

This Isn't Poker

Every service member has a choice to make in an environment that becomes more competitive. You can:

- **Keep your cards close**, conceal your leadership talents, hoard resources for your own team, and stand idly by as adjacent leaders falter … all in hopes of looking good at the expense of those around you.
- Or, you can **show your hand to the entire table**, share your tips and lessons, publicize your failings, volunteer for extra missions, and be generous with your time and resources.

Here's a key question for you: Which subordinate do you think your boss wants on the team?

I don't really need to answer that question because we all know that the best teams are made up of selfless people who care about enabling others and serving the organization. They know that everyone will be better off when everyone is performing better. So, they share knowledge, align efforts, and support others, even at the expense of their own advantage.

Whose Team Are You Serving?

Some people believe they won't get any of the credit if they show their hand to everyone else. This belief is shortsighted. **People who devote time to improving those around them cannot help but be noticed in a positive way.** And good talent shared prolifically cannot remain a secret. The real benefit will come when your boss sees his entire team strengthened by your efforts, not just *your* team.

Putting It Into Practice

Here are some ways in which military leaders can respond to the increasingly competitive environment by building the teams around them:

- Share EVERY good idea you have.
- Publicize failures that other units might also fall victim to (and subsequent lessons learned). This is particularly important for serious incidents or deaths, where key indicators often pointed to a tragic event but went unnoticed.
- Send out staff products that are making a difference for your unit.
- Share your policy letters and leadership philosophy.
- CC your teammates when emailing your commander about an important topic.
- Before you engage your commander on a topic, consult your fellow leaders to make sure you're on the same page. (This not only gives you a sanity check on your ideas, but presents a unified front to the commander.)
- Invite other teams to attend your morale, competition, and family events.
- Invite them to your professional development events, too.
- Volunteer your unit to take the less-desirable tasks that come down from higher up.

- Be the first to offer resources like ammunition and equipment when other units are in a bind.
- Share your training and live-fire ranges at every opportunity.
- Volunteer to provide Observer/Controller coverage for adjacent units that are conducting important training.
- Coach your subordinate key staff members to be personable, patient, and forgiving with other staffs, particularly higher headquarters.

What Becoming a Parent Taught Me About Leadership (Part 1)

In the months before having our first child, I captured some thoughts about how I thought becoming a parent would change me. Of course I knew it would be a *"crucible"* —a test or trial that causes defining and lasting change—but how would it alter who I was as a military leader? Would I view my role differently? Would I react to deployment orders with less stoicism when I have little ones to leave behind? Would I treat Soldiers differently?

I was sure to get these answers (and plenty more) with the birth of our two daughters. Below are excerpts from what I predicted I'd learn as a new father. Afterwards, I'll elaborate on the myriad of other ways in which having children has changed me as a leader.

Responsibility

"I anticipate that becoming a father will most impact me by opening up a new, uncharted arena of responsibility. In some ways it is like becoming a commander, where one day I am only accountable for my Army laptop and the next day I am responsible for every aspect of a 270-person organization."

Comfort Zone

"Raising a child will realign my notion of what is important and trivialize beliefs and actions I had previously held sacrosanct. Sleep, workout schedule, morning routine, finances, entertainment preferences, and household cleanliness will all be modified. In any other situation, making such changes to lifestyle would require applied discipline, but I anticipate that any hesitation or resistance I might feel will be overcome by an internal, innate motivation to ensure the best childhood for our son or daughter. This crucible will be like no other because the child instantly becomes priority number one."

Example

"Fatherhood will be a crucible of example setting. My actions, words, attitudes, and behaviors will no longer influence only my wife but also an extremely impressionable, malleable, and observant little person. My example will be both intentional and unintentional, impacting him or her on conscious and subconscious levels. This change will inspire me to further scrutinize how I lead myself and my family. And I believe that these revelations will affect my concept of Army leadership, as well."

Perspective of Soldiers

"Primarily, I expect that this crucible of becoming a parent will add an aspect of awareness to my performance as a leader. I will be less likely to view Soldiers as simply 'duty-performers' and instead gain an appreciation of them as sons and daughters of fellow parents. I have previously held this viewpoint during my time as a leader, but I predict that the influence will be stronger. My sense of compassion and empathy may deepen as well."

Operational Risk

"From an objective standpoint, these changes also have the potential to alter my concept of operational risk assessment. One might call it a 'baby bias.' Will I opt for a less daring course of action because I am more sensitive to the mortality of the mission? Will a fear of facing a grieving parent affect my willingness to put their sons and daughters at risk? My friends and family say that becoming a parent will change everything; but how expansive an influence will those changes have?"

What Becoming a Parent Taught Me About Leadership (Part 2)

Previously, I revealed a few of the ways in which I thought becoming a parent would change me. I anticipated the obvious, like that a new baby would transform my daily routine and thrust me out of my comfort zone, and that I would instantly become a persistent example of right and wrong to this little being. I predicted that having a child would also influence how I interact with Soldiers and perform as a leader. Turns out, I was only scratching the surface of lessons that parenthood can teach a leader.

Empathy

Definition: "*The ability to understand and share the feelings of another.*" As a leader in multiple organizations, I'd helped plenty of Soldiers navigate family difficulties, but having children brought an acute awareness of the challenges of raising a family while serving in the military. I simply could not comprehend the experience until I lived it myself. Family problems grab a Soldier's attention like nothing else and will continue to distract him/her from the mission until resolved. Family challenges also impact Soldier resilience, which is already tough to maintain given the daily job requirements and deployments. As a leader, I've learned to surge assets to help a Soldier with family problems.

Lesson: Understand that family is priority for everyone. Don't discard a subordinate's problem as minor because it wouldn't be a big deal for your family. Give them the benefit of the doubt, the assistance, and the freedom to solve the problem. That's what leaders do.

Value Family Time

It was easy to stay late at the office when there was no one waiting at home. I actually equated long work hours with productivity, sacrifice, and admirable work ethic. Now, long work hours mean missing out on quality moments that are irreplaceable. After having children, I get edgy toward the late afternoon because I want to be at home with my girls. Thankfully for the folks I'm leading, this anxiousness usually overcomes me and I just leave the office, which means that they can leave the office too. I also have an appreciation for followers who ask to take time for family events.

Lesson: There's not a lot of routine work that should keep you late. Stop pretending that working late is a badge of honor and commit to being more productive within reasonable work hours.

Include Single Soldiers

Having children made me realize how many military programs/events are oriented towards families and not single service members. It's not intentional; it's just that the majority of military leaders have families and many have forgotten what it's like to be single. I had a recent commander who made sure to include activities for single Soldiers in every unit event and campaigned for them to attend.

Lesson: It's not the leader's job to give every subordinate something to do, but it is a leader's job to provide equal opportunity across the ranks, which will build cohesion.

Get Your Affairs in Order

After children, my wife and I found an urgency to get our administrative affairs straight. We updated our wills and selected a designated guardian in case something happened to both of us. And we ensured that our life insurance policies were accurate. After this process, I paid more attention to how my Soldiers were handling their affairs and engaged them to ensure they weren't pencil-whipping deployment documents like wills and next of kin notification documents. It paid off, as I found that many Soldiers had outdated or incorrect information and hadn't taken the time to consider some of these serious topics.

Lesson: No one likes to do the administrivia of life. Taking care of followers means helping them do the things they *should* be doing ... that goes for both official and unofficial business.

Pick Your Battles

My toddlers teach me this lesson every day now. There is plenty that they do that I don't like, but trying to reason my way through a tantrum is hopeless. So, my wife and I do a lot of ignoring. We prevent dangerous acts and correct mean behavior or disobedience, but the rest we let go. The connection to organizational leadership is clear, but I didn't understand this lesson until I had to live it at home.

Lesson: Not every problem deserves your attention. The most efficient way of solving problems might not be the most effective way. Subordinates can learn a lot from having the freedom to figure out problems on their own. Avoid the temptation to rush in and fix everything.

Plan Ahead

My wife would say that I have a long way to go with this lesson, but having children has shown me that *everything takes 5 times as long as I think it wil,l* and if we want to get out the door at 9 am, we have to start getting ready at 7. (Funny how Clausewitz's lesson on friction reveals itself at home on a Saturday morning.) This reality has had a direct impact on how I plan operational timelines and anticipate friction. It also showed me that preparations and rehearsals are essential for a successful event.

Lesson: Leaders cannot effectively make their own plans on short-notice or expect an organization to turn on a dime. Give members of your organization more time than you think they'll need, even if that means shortening your own staff's planning time.

Don't Forget to Teach the Basics

It's amazing how clear this lesson becomes when you've got a person in your life who knows absolutely nothing about anything! Having to teach a little girl to use a fork has taught me that even the most rudimentary lessons are appreciated by someone. New Soldiers and officers may enter service with zeal and motivation, but they have no real-world experience and rely on leaders to provide a working knowledge of the profession.

Lesson: As leaders progress in rank and responsibility, they take more and more skills for granted. Reach back to old lessons and pass those on to the younger generation—they need to hear them.

Clarify Your Communication

While I am incredibly thankful for them, our two daughters brought some noise and chaos to our home. I've found that it's become very easy for my wife and I to talk right past each other, saying plenty but not communicating. (I'll admit that I'm always working on my listening skills.) Sometimes we have to physically get each other's attention to get a point across. It's not unlike trying to share information in the midst of a combat event, where the abundance of distractions makes for a short attention span and limited comprehension.

Lesson: Identify the moments that require clear communication and emplace protocols to ensure the right people get the information they need. Leaders must protect their ability to remain above the fray and provide perspective during chaos.

Make Time for Reflection and Personal Growth

Being slightly introverted, I used to recharge my mental batteries reading a book in the anonymity of a Starbucks. Unplugging from the daily commitments changed my perspective and facilitated problem solving and insight. But with the flood of activities and responsibilities that accompany children, "quiet time" seems like a distant memory.

The transition showed me that reflective time is crucial for personal and professional growth, which is nonnegotiable for a leader. If I wanted it to happen, I needed to make quiet time a priority and carve out the space for it. For me, the 5 o'clock hour is where I get my reading and writing done, which means I've had to get to bed earlier. But if I don't find this time, I won't grow ... which means those I lead won't grow.

Lesson: Children bring plenty of reasons to devalue the recovery and personal growth that comes with quiet time. Leaders, however, have a mandate to grow. Find a balance that sets the conditions for your personal development and teach those around you to do the same.

Make Time for Physical Fitness

The same goes for your health. Kids can steal the time you once had to workout and you won't notice it until 40 pounds later. And the military doesn't give you a pass on fitness because you have kids now.

Lesson: You can't take care of your family (or your followers) if you don't take care of yourself. Fitness is mandatory, just do it!

"This is Harder Than Ranger School ..."

Five days after the birth of our second child ... at about 3:30am ... I actually muttered this confession to my wife: "This is harder than Ranger School." The constant responsibility and every-two-hour feeding schedule had broken me worse than any rucksack ever did.

Lesson: Just like Ranger School ... Don't quit!

Nine Misguided Reasons to go to Selection

Whether you're battling the crashing waves on Coronado Beach, slogging out mile after mile in the sugar sands of Fort Bragg, or trudging your way up and down the deceptively steep Appalachian Mountains, attending selection for one of America's elite special operations force units is a gauntlet of physical and mental endurance.

The fitness demands exceed what you could have possibly hoped to train for. You face each day not knowing which of your professional (and personal) talents you'll be called upon to validate. Your career ambitions—and often your life's goals—rest on the assessment of operators who have *forgotten* more about combat than you'll ever know.

But if you make it through … if they accept you … you're set. You're on the team! You can go no higher. And can brag for the rest of your life about how you were "one of them," earning instant respect in any circle.

… Right?

"Selection Never Stops"

Selection is full of people who think that making the roster is the hardest step, when in fact it's the very, very beginning. The intense specialty training that follows, then the operational tempo that today's target-rich environment demands, make selection look like a vacation.

Every day is a test to stay in SOF, to improve skills that were perfected years ago, to maintain fitness for any fight in any environment, to envision solutions for unknown tactical challenges to come. SOF units rest their success on the tenet that one must continually verify the skills required to win.

Operators have a phrase that endures their tenure: "*Selection never stops.*"

The Wrong Reasons

So, "*because life will be a lot easier*" is not a good reason to try out for SOF. And in an effort to stir a little introspection for those interested in taking the walk, here are a few other reasons that should **not** be driving factors in one's quest to join the ranks of the elite:

- **To validate your personal or professional worth.** This reason is very common, yet no one will admit it. Lots of folks apply for SOF because they need it to justify their military service. The mindset is usually phrased like this, "*I just have to go and find out if I have what it takes.*" People with this mindset aren't happy in their current professional (sometimes personal) situation and need acceptance from the toughest units in the military to fill the void. It won't work. A military unit can't validate a man or give him purpose.

- **To see if you can physically handle it.** People with this notion are shortsighted and won't last. Physical fitness is just the starting point of a life in SOF. It's the very first gate you must survive, not the last. Mental agility, creativity, and intellectual fortitude make up so much more of an operator's life than fitness.

- **You don't want to be in the "big Army/Navy" anymore.** Running away from the conventional force is a prime motivator for joining SOF. Folks think that life is just *so much better over there*, that there are no unit problems or bureaucratic nonsense. Again, shortsighted. People are people. Every organization has good ones and not-so-good ones. Drama and people problems are unavoidable facts of leadership environments. SOF is no different.

- **You think leading conventional troops isn't important enough.** Similarly, some self-absorbed people think that conventional

Soldiers/Sailors aren't worth their effort to lead, that they're substandard service members. They don't appreciate what an awesome opportunity it is to lead service members, regardless of the unit. Then when these people fail selection, they let their resentful attitude hamper their performance, short-changing their unit and themselves.

- **You're tired of playing by the rules or wearing a uniform.** Younger officers and NCOs often get enamored with the idea of having increased responsibility, less oversight, and fewer conventional restrictions. They want to be in the "cool guy club." I can assure you that an ardent desire to grow a beard has never been sufficient, or even helpful, in passing SOF selection. A currently serving operator I know confirmed, "*Yes, we wear uniforms, go to mandatory annual training, and take DA Photos. We're still part of the service.*"

- **You think you will get more time at home.** Four month deployments sound nice, but the reality is that SOF units have been deploying 4-on, 4-off (or more) for 15 years straight, and to more theaters. And they will continue to deploy long after the conventional forces leave country. Operators don't get more time at home, because when they're not deployed, they're training. People associate "big boy rules" with free time ... not the case in SOF.

- **You think you'll be an instant operator if you pass selection.** Refer to the above point that *selection never stops.* You never "arrive" in SOF—you only strive to grow to a higher level of lethality. Just like Basic Training, selection is designed to see if candidates have the foundational skills to *potentially* handle the rigors of life on the other side. There's no guarantee that anyone will pass the training that follows selection, and frankly, SOF units have such a faithful adherence to the standard that they'd rather fail everybody than put an unqualified operator on the teams.

- **SOF has higher promotion rates and more command opportunities.** Good-on the person who can get through selection and training motivated by career advancement. It doesn't happen often. The facts are that the promotion rates are very similar to conventional units and there are far fewer command opportunities in SOF than elsewhere. To command in SOF, you have to be the most lethal, agile, reliable, and consistent leader in a pool of similarly talented peers. It's no picnic. And it's no reason to take the walk.

- As my good friend in Army SOF said, *"Going to SOF doesn't make you a hero."* You have to earn everything. And when you do valorous things in SOF units, it's commonplace. Humility is pervasive there, which starves egos looking for attention. The "Quiet Professionals" attitude is alive and well, so don't think that joining SOF will get you free beers for the rest of your life.

One Right Reason

There's really only one reason to try out for SOF … and one that the evaluators are specifically screening for. **Selfless service**. It sounds like this:

> *"I've gained some skillsets in my short career. I want to offer them in units that have the highest impact for my Nation. I don't know if they're what SOF is looking for, but I'm willing to push myself past exhaustion to make them available."*

To get in the right mindset, you should become stoically dispassionate about your endeavor to join the SOF ranks. Accept that SOF units are looking for a very narrow bandwidth of talent and that although you meet all the qualifications, you might not be the right person for the job. That doesn't make you less of a leader or a failure. It just means that your skillsets aren't specifically tailored for success in SOF.

And here's the reality: If you aren't up to their standard, you don't *want* to be there! What's worse than not passing selection is making it through only to find out that you never really had the requisite skills, and consequently put people at risk. Not cool.

Section 2
Sharpen Your Skills

How to Write a Change of Command Speech

Chances are you've been in one of the following situations: a member of a formation suffering under a long change of command speech; an audience member embarrassed for the speaking commander because his speech is really bad; or a soon-to-be ex-commander staring at a blank page on the morning of your own departure speech. Sound familiar?

Don't worry, we've all been there. The change of command speech is important but it can sneak up on you in the distracted days before the big event. Here are some thoughts to consider as you prepare for the transition. There are sections for Incoming Commanders, Outgoing Commanders, and some general tips.

Going Into Command

- Keep it short (2–3 minutes)
- Introduction: Welcome the guests, but don't run down the entire laundry list of those attending. You'll be the third person to speak, and the guests will feel plenty-welcomed by then.
- Be sure to thank:
    - The Chain of Command for the opportunity.
    - The Outgoing Commander & his/her family.
    - Your spouse & family.
    - The troops, and express gratitude for the honor of joining their team.
    - Write two sentences about the privilege to command and how you're looking forward to what the future will bring.

- Do not say, *"All policies and procedures remain in effect."* First, it sounds ridiculous and cliché. Second, there's no regulation or policy requirement to do so, nor is there any expectation that Army regulations and UCMJ are no longer applicable if you don't say those seven words at your change of command. And finally, it's not true. You're going to change every policy letter when you resign it under your name. And, heaven forbid, you might actually change some things because you're the commander and you have the authority to do so.

Leaving Command

- Keep it short(ish) (8–10 minutes).
- Introduction: Go ahead and thank the key guests for attending. Welcome General Officers and equivalent Sergeants Major by name. Welcome your commander by name. Welcome all others by group, unless an individual stands out in some significant way (Medal of Honor recipient or "Honorary Colonel of the Unit").
- Include some mention of why we serve, and of the concepts of duty, honor, and sacrifice.
- Honor fallen/wounded Soldiers, as appropriate.
- Relive the story of your time in command, but from the Soldiers' perspective, not yours.
- Retell some stories using individual names (e.g., "The company's success during NTC grew out of the individual efforts of men like squad leader SSG Goldman, who single-handedly breached the wire obstacle on the final objective.").
- Thank:
    - Your Chain of Command
    - The unit for their sacrifice
    - Your staff and higher headquarters staff for putting up with you
    - Adjacent and supporting/attached units as necessary
    - Your key staff members
    - Your senior enlisted leader
    - Your spouse

General Tips

- Rehearse your speech NO LESS THAN 10 TIMES!!
- Get feedback from your peers and spouse on content and timing.
- Don't ad-lib unless you are a gifted orator or an extrovert who can carry a crowd.
- Type your speech in big font and wide paragraph spacing, put the pages into sheet protectors, and prepare them in a three-ring binder to use at the podium.
- Have a second fully functioning binder in case the Adjutant loses the primary one.
- If you're cool, consider putting the formation At Ease.
- DO NOT NOT NOT forget to thank your spouse! There is no chance that you would have been as successful as you were without him/her, so you should probably state that fact publicly.
- And finally ... please don't cry.

14 Simple Ways to Connect with Your People

Leaders who find ways to connect with their people are the ones who build great teams, inspire the best performance, and rise to positions of influence when others wane. If you look back on your career, you'll likely observe that the most impactful leaders were the ones who made a personal connection with you.

Maybe it was keen professional mentorship, timely advice during adversity, or a personality trait that invited trust. Sometimes there's no pinpointing it … just an intangible feeling that makes it easy to follow a person.

In the culture of busyness that we face today, it's distressingly easy to ignore the personal side of leadership. **But trust will never develop without a personal connection between leader and follower.** And without trust, an organization will be confined to a transactional environment of mediocre results and melancholy people.

This is a list of simple ways that leaders can make a personal connection. These are the kinds of engagements that cause followers (and their spouses) to walk away saying, *"Wow, that was very thoughtful of him"* or *"She didn't have to do that, but we really appreciated it."* These are also methods that your team members and subordinates will admire and adopt for their own leadership profile.

Make the Personal Connection

- **Learn their first names.** This is a must from day one. The days of stoic military professional stiffness are over. Today's generation

70

expects a personal connection. Plus, you shouldn't go to war with someone if you don't know their first name.

- **Learn their spouses' names.** In a similar vein, learning spouses' names is a critical first step to conveying that you care about the *entire* team, not just the service member. Develop a system or a cheat sheet, if you must, and recruit your own spouse for help.

- **Go to the hospital.** I can't overstate how important this is. If a team member or spouse has a baby or is hospitalized, supporting them in person at the hospital has a profound impact. I still remember the three people who came to visit us when our second daughter was born, and one of them was my Regimental Commander.

- **Give them paternity leave.** Don't think for a second that your unit's work is more important than the support a husband can give his wife in the weeks after childbirth. Giving them time off to get settled has a lifetime impact.

- **Send holiday/anniversary cards.** Ok, after you get the first names down and visit them in the hospital, follow up by celebrating the season and recognizing their big life moments. Cards are easy and reinforce the team concept outside of the office.

- **Call their spouse on promotion day.** This happened to me recently and I thought it was a classy touch. The promotion list came out and my boss called me into his office for a chat. After a few minutes, he asked if my wife was busy and proceeded to dial her up on speakerphone. Then he took the time to congratulate both of us and thank her for everything she did to help make it happen. It was a personal connection that resonated with both of us.

- **Send a thank you card on a significant milestone.** I knew a leader who mailed thank you cards home to spouses just prior to a unit leave period, thanking them for supporting their spouse during the surge of recent activity. As a bonus, in the card he made sure to praise their husband's good work, which put a few points on the board at home.

Make the Professional Connection

- **Give them the Why.** Nothing inspires followers like knowing the purpose behind the mission. There is a stark difference between the leader who says, *"Here's why this is important"* and the one who says, *"Just get it done."*

- **Actually <u>do</u> counseling with them.** If there's a personal activity that military leaders routinely fail at, it's counseling. When we skip counseling, we're basically saying, *"You're doing good enough work for me not to yell at you, but I'm too busy to tell you how you're really doing or tell you how you could improve. So good luck."* Counseling doesn't have to be a big deal. Just sit down in an informal setting and talk about Strengths, Weaknesses, and the Way Ahead.

- **Help them prepare for a promotion board.** Preparing your file for a promotion board isn't rocket science, but it does take experience and attention to detail that junior service members might not have. A leader who puts personal time into helping subordinates with their careers will leave a lasting positive impression and prepare those talented subordinates for continued success.

- **Ask for input about an area that's outside their lane.** Ask a subordinate team member for advice on a topic that's above their pay grade, then watch them stand a little taller and willingly connect. Use this technique when drafting an email to your own boss or preparing an important brief. You might find that you get some fresh perspective on your work, too.

- **Highlight them in public.** Peer recognition is incredibly powerful for committing individuals to the team. Make it a point to recognize hard workers in public, especially when their performance was behind the scenes.

- **Give them unplanned time off ... and time off when they really need it.** If members of your team went above and beyond, reward them with some time off. And when your people are facing a life struggle, give them space from work to get through it. You can bet that higher-up leaders will take an afternoon off to get the car fixed, so make sure you give the same to the troops.

- **Receive them like rock stars, then back off.** This one happened to us and we appreciated it immensely. When you get new members to your unit, make a deliberate effort to give them the red carpet treatment. Keep in touch as they move to town. Meet them upon arrival with a gift basket full of the necessities for the first couple days. Follow up to ensure they get signed-in and that there are no administrative hassles you can help fix.

Then— and this is important—tell them not to come to work until *pictures are hanging on the walls.* It's all too common for units to make their new people feel like the world is going to end if they don't start work the day after the boxes arrive at the house. Leaders need to realize that the unit will continue marching right along even if this person doesn't come in for another week. This is the crucial first impression, and an opportunity to show that you care about family. How you treat these new team members will determine how they perform while they're on your team, and more importantly, whether or not they reenlist to continue service.

Making a difference in your people's lives doesn't have to be a complicated process. With a little creativity, leaders can easily find ways to convey gratitude for their team members' service and sacrifice, as well as that of their family. Make that connection and you will be a leader with lasting influence.

Sleep That Sabotages Leadership

A Harvard Business Review article from 2014, "Your Abusive Boss Is Probably an Insomniac," summarized the findings from a study published in the *Academy of Management Journal*. The researchers studied 88 leaders and their teams to find out if the leaders' sleep habits affected performance at work.

The result? You guessed it; leaders don't get enough sleep. But there's a twist:

> We found that daily leader sleep quality, but not *quantity*, influenced the leader's self-control and abusive supervision behavior, and ultimately the degree to which his or her subordinates were engaged in their work that day. It is not clear why sleep quantity did not have the effect we predicted, but the effect for sleep quality was very clear; a given leader engaged in more jerky boss behavior after a poor night of sleep than a good night of sleep, and this influenced his or her subordinates to disengage from work.

So, we should pay attention to *how well we sleep* in addition to *how much we sleep*. And it turns out from the study that the poor sleep quality didn't just impair the leader, it affected subordinate behavior as well:

> Perhaps what is most interesting about these findings is that leader sleep influenced subordinate outcomes. Although most of us have some appreciation that our own sleep influences our own behaviors and outcomes, not many people would expect someone else's sleep to

influence one's own behavior. But this is precisely what we found; **leader sleep quality influenced subordinate work engagement**. Thus, if leaders want their subordinates to be truly engaged, they should start by looking at their own sleep.

What About Military Leaders?

Unquestionably, the military is a sleep-challenged profession. Combat operations and intense training events provide ample opportunities to sacrifice sleep. We're good at driving-on despite fatigue (to a point …). But we have lots of leaders who also figure out a way to short themselves of a good night's rest *in garrison*, when no bullets are flying.

But if sleep quality/quantity affects team behavior, shouldn't we consider it lack of discipline not to arrive at the point of departure in a peak state of performance?

We leaders need to take a hard look at our own physiological states. It's cool to be "the rough commander who has a bit of an edge and a temper from time to time," until you start destroying the very thing you're responsible for.

Leaders carry more psychological burden than other members and need to shape their environment to maximize performance. Establish wake-up criteria so your people know when to rouse you. Set a cut-off time for work-related activity so you can relax your body and mind before lights-out. Put some effort into assessing your lifestyle activities like sleep time, hydration, caffeine intake, fitness, and food. They all play a part in shaping your work behavior.

Achieving Effects with Your Boss, Part 1: First Impressions

On the list of items that leaders should care about, there are few higher than achieving effects with your boss. (Above it, one might list *achieving the mission* and *building trust with your subordinates*.) The purpose is clear enough, to ensure alignment while creating opportunities for your own team. But leaders often place too much emphasis inward and downward during their key leadership time, and neglect to satisfy higher headquarters' goals.

What's more, achieving effects with your boss is a tough balancing act. Too assertive and you come off as pushy while alienating yourself from your peers. Too passive and you won't gain the influence necessary to achieve your goals as a leader.

This series will provide you with the why, when, and how to engage your boss in ways that support his goals while achieving effects for your team. This one, *First Impressions*, is all about starting off on the right foot. And not to put undue pressure on you, but the process of gaining influence with your boss starts before you even arrive at the unit.

Preparation

Congratulations! You just found out you're going into a leadership position! It's time to go to work.

Do some immediate research to **orient yourself to the new terrain.** What's the unit's mission, motto, history, and task organization? What is the training or deployment glide path? Find out who will be on your team when you get there and who your boss will be. Do all this quickly— you don't want to sound ignorant if a senior leader (or worse, your future boss) calls to congratulate you.

You'll obviously need to know a lot about your future team and how it operates, but in the context of this section, let's focus on the boss. You need to **educate yourself on who you will be working for.** Google your future boss. Read articles he may have written. Read his biography on the unit home page. Talk to peers who may have worked with him in the past. Talk to mentors about the leadership environment you're walking into.

This preparation will shape your initial communication with him and set conditions for your first meeting. It will also give you an idea of how the leader is perceived by those outside the chain of command, which could be important knowledge in the future.

The First Round

The next step is important. You need to send an introductory note. What it says is less important than seizing a classy opportunity to show the boss you are excited to join the team and still recognize time-honored military traditions. You can do this by email, snail mail, or a combination where you type and sign a letter, then scan and attach it to an email. Either way, the most important part is to **keep it short and to the point!** This isn't the time to give your life's story, detail your leadership philosophy, or reveal your childhood goal to someday be General Patton.

Give a short intro, thank her for the opportunity to lead, take a sentence to tell her about your family, and inform her when you'll be arriving at the new post or moving to your position. You can include a paragraph about your professional experience, but be brief—your new boss will have access to your file. Be sure to include your contact information below your signature block.

Arrival

In the past, hopefully you have arrived at new installations to be greeted by a sponsor or someone from the team you're joining who will help you get settled. This changes as you become a more senior leader. Your arrival becomes more visible to the command (especially if you are going *into* command). **It's entirely possible for your boss to be waiting at the doorstep of your new home as you finish your 10-hour drive.** Think through what to do if this happens. You don't need to be at the top of your game, but you also don't want to be unshaven and visibly angry at your kids.

If you do arrive with no fanfare, be sure to send a quick note to either the boss or his immediate staff to let him know you made it. Update him with the move-in schedule so he knows when you'll be available, which might also protect your family time to get settled. (Quick tip: If you are a leader, be sure to give your new team members plenty of time to move into the new home. There's nothing worse than trying to learn a new job when the house is a disaster and your spouse is left to deal with it. My guidance: *"Don't come to work until you have pictures hung and it feels like a home."*)

Initial Meeting

Now, let's take a look at the first official meeting. It may be an official counseling session or just an informal, *"Welcome, step into the office."* If you are coming onto the team without a specified position yet (like as a junior staff Captain or a Sergeant First Class hoping to get a platoon), recognize that **this meeting may also serve as an interview** to see where you'll fit on the team.

Regardless, your goals for the first encounter should be:

1. Walk away with a clear sense of the boss's priorities and expectations.
2. Give her an *accurate* sense of who you are and how you will perform. (It's a bad idea to put on a show up front without the skill to back it up later.)

3. Make it evident that you recognize your place on *her team*, and aren't solely focused on how you will lead *your team*.

4. Figure out the way ahead. What changes are happening in the unit? When will you move into position? What can you work on in the meantime?

All bosses will have different methods, but yours may also want to see your file, including your Record Brief (or curriculum vitae), previous evaluation reports, and perhaps some command-related documents like your Command Guidance or Policy Letters. Consider carrying those with you in the first few days at the unit.

Also, **rehearse how to tell your story.** The boss wants to get to know you, but you're not going to become best friends at this first meeting. Be brief, sincere, and humble. It's likely that your boss has already done research on you, too, so you don't need to go bragging for ten minutes about how great you were in your last assignment. Have an answer for what you want to do *after* the upcoming assignment and how long you plan to serve.

Finally, **DO NOT forget to talk about your family.** They are a critical part of your leadership experience. Make sure she knows that you recognize that.

The First 90 Days

The first 90 days is not the time for the change crusade. Similar to the advice that says "*Don't try to change everything as soon as you take over an organization,*" you should also avoid trying to change your *boss's* organization when you're still new to the team. And be aware that subordinates may bombard you with problems that "must be fixed!"

If the issues that surface involve decisions your boss has made, **stop and do your homework before storming into his office.** (You may have the authority of command, but building credibility takes time.) Check the problem against his stated priorities and talk to your peers and advisors. This will give you an informed and accurate perspective of the leadership environment your boss has created.

Then take time to identify what areas you can realistically influence in the coming months and years, and strategically plan a method of engagement. (Later, I'll share some tips on how to engage your boss when you are trying to change a policy or reverse a decision.)

In these beginning months, **make it abundantly clear that you understand your boss's priorities and are in alignment with them.** Answer his emails quickly, respond to requests for information, integrate his command guidance into yours, complete the unit training requirements that come down from higher, and send him updates on progress, even when they're not required.

Finally, make it clear to your boss that you are open to honest and candid feedback about your performance. Some people aren't comfortable with making performance corrections, even some bosses. But during this beginning phase, you definitely want to get back on course quickly if you happen to veer off.

Closeout

Pulling it all together: Achieving effects with your boss begins early in your relationship. Start off right by doing your research, sending a short introduction email, intentionally preparing for the first meeting, aligning your priorities, and resisting the urge to spend all your capital on changing everything right away.

Achieving Effects with Your Boss, Part 2: Intentional Engagement

Spotlight Ranger. That's the label service members use to characterize people who put in average performance day to day, then put on a show whenever the boss is around. Soldiers see right through them and they earn little respect in the unit.

While you must at all costs avoid becoming a spotlight ranger (i.e., dedicate yourself to superb performance regardless of the audience), you don't want to miss an opportunity to showcase your unit's good work to your boss. Part 1 focused on how to start off on the right foot with a new boss. This section looks at how to engage during three types of opportunities you will encounter during your tenure as leader.

When to Engage

Success in any endeavor depends largely on seizing opportunities. Engagements come and go throughout each day and the best leaders recognize and prepare for the engagements that will provide the greatest return for their team and themselves. I once had a Command Sergeant Major who gave his commander this advice on day one, *"Focus on meeting higher headquarters' priorities so that you can gain maneuver space for us to do what we think is important."*

Opportunities to achieve effects with your boss will include three types of engagements: *Touchpoints*, *Planned Encounters*, and *Decisive Engagements*.

Touchpoints

Touchpoints are the informal, unplanned, everyday events with your boss that are typically not on the calendar. Emails, phone calls, and drop-by visits are touchpoints. Secondhand information is also a touchpoint, although you may not be present to witness it. **Touchpoints are important because they inform your boss's opinion about your day-to-day leadership.** How do you handle routine problems? Are you informed about your own unit's activity? Do you *live* the boss's priorities or only focus on them occasionally?

Planned Encounters

These are your meetings and scheduled events with your boss. It's the training, staff, or maintenance meeting. It's the Monday morning run to catch up, as well as the Friday afternoon closeout huddle to wrap up. Planned encounters are likely where you'll spend the most time with your boss and will often include your adjacent unit leaders. **These opportunities will reveal your personal preparation and your unit's staff capability.**

Decisive Engagements

Decisive engagements are your championship playoff games. They are decisive because they set the tone for your time as leader and could (for better or worse) overshadow other work that you and your unit are doing. A change of command is a decisive engagement, as are major training events. Hosting a unit-wide social function is a decisive engagement. Any event that your *boss's boss* will be at is a decisive engagement. Depending on your boss, your periodic counseling could be decisive. **You must nail these opportunities.**

How to Engage

Remember, **every engagement with your boss is a chance to achieve some type of effect for you and your organization.** Those desired effects don't materialize during casual conversation; they form from deliberate thought and careful revision. They shape the environment that will allow you and your unit to achieve success.

Depending on your leadership environment, determining when and how to engage can be challenging. Your best advice will come from your senior enlisted advisor, your mentors, and your spouse. Beyond their tailored recommendations, here's how to achieve effects when you get the opportunity:

- **Prioritize priorities.** What are your boss's priorities? What are your priorities? How can you clearly communicate that you are supporting *her* priorities? You can accomplish a hundred "good ideas" a day, but if you don't fulfill the one or two priorities your boss cares about, you'll fail. **Show that you are nested with her efforts,** which you can certainly do in creative ways that give your unit character apart from others. (Tip: Knowing your boss's priorities from memory will prime you for the touchpoint moments.)

- **Pick subordinate team members to highlight.** Talking about subordinate accomplishments instead of your own is one of those classy habits that separate good leaders from great leaders. Whether it's in a public setting or in a private meeting, it's ok to talk about what your unit leaders are doing to make a difference, especially if it achieves one of your boss's priorities. Specifically, **pick one leader that your boss senior rates and one or two Soldiers that recently stood out.** Highlight them during a public meeting or during a speech. It'll put them on the radar and reflect positively on the unit as a whole. Unit visits are also a good time to ask your boss to present awards to outstanding performers.

- **Share instances of adjacent unit cooperation.** People who devote time to improving those around them cannot help but be noticed in a positive way. When you get time with the boss, especially in unit meetings where your peers are present, talk about the good stuff that is happening between the units. Highlight how you are strengthening *across* the teams, which is to say, "Sir, here is how we are building *your* team."

- **Comment on areas of growth.** Show your boss that you and the unit are moving forward. Discuss some key areas that you are trying to improve, either from recent training feedback or through strategic planning. This will make it evident that you are in tune with your unit's performance and are personally involved in strengthening its capability.

- **Create more opportunities.** Not every leader naturally gets out of the office to visit the troops. If that's your boss, you have to take the initiative. Scour your calendar for events that show off what your team is doing and invite your boss.

- **Prepare and rehearse.** You'll have to wing most of the touchpoint moments, but you'll achieve greater effects if you put some time into preparing for the planned events like meetings and functions. Create talking points, run them by your trusted advisors, align them with your fellow leaders left and right, anticipate questions and branch topics, and practice.

- **Win the Super Bowl!** For decisive engagements like unit visits by senior leaders or major training events, you have no option but to nail it. Direct numerous meetings to review the plan and allow five times as much time as you think you'll need to prepare. Dive into the details, challenge assumptions, question the availability of resources, and plan multiple dress rehearsals. **Being a meticulous leader is ok in these moments.** You don't want some simple oversight like technical difficulties or protocol slights to distract your boss from the point of the event. Get honest feedback by asking someone outside the organization to scrub the plan and watch the rehearsals. **Your goal? Send a clear message in a frictionless environment to achieve specific effects.**

Closeout

Encounters with your boss will range from quick emails to hours-long visits at the range. You must be ready to purposefully engage to achieve effects that 1) meet your boss's priorities, 2) highlight your team's accomplishments, 3) build the team across, and 4) create more opportunities.

The next section in this series will deal with how to engage your boss in the different types of decision situations you might face. Influencing her to change her mind on a policy requires a different approach than seeking to gain approval on one of your own initiatives. We'll look at how to prepare for those and other types of encounters.

Achieving Effects with Your Boss, Part 3: Decision Time

So far in the Achieving Effects with Your Boss series, we've covered how to make the right first impression and how to engage your boss with intention. Now that you're comfortable with the leadership environment your boss has established, it's time to discuss how to influence his decision making to achieve effects for you, your team, and the greater organization.

Disclaimer

Be warned ... We are wading into potentially dangerous territory in the effort to influence your boss's decision making. You need to evaluate the type of leadership your boss is exhibiting before you start suggesting changes. Most leaders welcome feedback and constructive suggestions to make the command better. But the wrong type of leader might punt you right outside the circle of trust if he thinks you're encroaching on his authority.

Why Seek a Decision?

Regardless, here are some reasons for which you might engage your boss for a decision:

- Seeking approval for an activity your unit will conduct
- Influencing the way in which your unit will fit into upcoming operations or events

- Attempting to change a policy that your boss has implemented or plans to implement
- Defending yourself or your unit in the wake of a negative incident
- Lobbying for a subordinate to take a key position on the boss's staff or receive a certain evaluation rating
- Gaining his endorsement for YOUR next job
- Requesting his action to correct an issue with his own staff

Check your intent

Your first step is to ensure your desire for change is grounded in the right motives and then to decide how big of a change you are seeking. Consider these questions:

- Will this change benefit you, your team, or the organization as a whole?
- Are your desires in line with what's good for your team?
- Is this a decision that can be reached and implemented within the boss's tenure?
- Is it short-term tactical or long-term strategic?
- Will it cause your boss to go against a policy or decision she's set before?
- Does she even have the authority to act, or must she go up the chain of command?

Check Your Engagement Methods

Next, figure out the best way to bring up your change idea. You've got a few options beyond just walking into the boss's office. Should you:

- Go it alone?
- Rally your own team behind it?
- Get adjacent unit/leader buy-in?
- Seek input from your mentors or other key brokers?
- Engage your boss's staff to feel out the topic first or shape conditions?

How you answer these questions will shape your plan of engagement, frame how you approach the problem, and set expectations about how quickly change might occur.

Consolidate Your Position

Before you take action to influence your environment, be clear about what is best for you and your organization. What do you really want from the boss? **What are the minimum conditions that would satisfy your intent?** If you must, develop talking points or an elevator pitch. You don't want casual chatter to commit you to a half-developed idea.

Map the Objective

Now it's time to develop an engagement strategy based on what type of decision you are seeking. If it's a long term effort, you may have to develop a phased plan to influence your boss. On the other hand, if he is the decision authority but the decision won't affect his organization, you may not need to invest a lot of time. Recognize that if you plan on seeking a decision that changes the course of your boss's organization or reverses a previous decision, you'll need to research your approach and gain some allies.

Rally the Troops

When you do enlist support for your cause, do so discretely with trusted peers and mentors. What's worse than the boss shooting down your proposal is that he thinks you're plotting something and not telling her. **Pitch your ideas to peers in adjacent units and earnestly seek their input.** Ask them to check the sanity of your plan, determine the risk involved, and offer alternate approaches. This process strengthens your argument and builds legitimacy.

Shape the Environment

Don't march into the boss's office just yet. Instead, ponder how you can shape her close-in environment to make your effort easier. It may help to float your ideas by her staff and senior advisors, who will know what she is thinking about the topic and maybe have a sense of whether it's a good time to bring it up.

Note: If you do approach other people or your boss's staff about the issue, be very clear that it's off the record and in draft form. You don't want one of them to mess up your engagement strategy by revealing it early.

Assault the Objective

When it's time to approach the boss with your request, choose the venue deliberately. Does the topic require a separate meeting or briefing? Should your fellow leaders be present? Maybe it's best to drop a hint in casual conversation or email then follow up later in a more formal setting. In any case, you'll have the best chance for a positive decision if you are in control of how your argument is presented.

Prepare your reasoning with a bottom line up front, bullet points to support your position, and counterarguments that may arise. Remember, your goal is to improve the overall capability of the entire team, so be open to legitimate criticism and view it as a way to improve your approach.

Take notes, confirm details, and follow up on actionable points. And if your boss isn't ready to commit to a decision during the first discussion, don't push her. Some leaders want to let new ideas marinate before fully engaging.

Follow Through

Make sure to thank your boss for her willingness to be persuaded. **There are plenty of leaders out there who want nothing to do with change or subordinate ideas.** If you are successful and your new decision requires action, get to work right away. Show that you're committed to producing tangible results, not just getting your way. Immediately schedule a follow-up meeting or update and communicate how the boss's decision has affected the organization. Again, your goal is the bigger team. If the decision ultimately turns out to have been a bad one, let your boss know, then go back to the drawing board.

Conclusion

Hopefully in this series, you can see that every encounter with your boss is an opportunity to move the ball down the field. Leaders don't have casual encounters with the boss, not when organizations are relying on them to create better conditions for success. The most successful leaders prioritize their efforts, plan their engagement methods, and are deliberate about leveraging their influence. That's what their people expect.

The Secret to a Blister-free Foot March

The Fort Benning summer heat baked around us as a crusty Sergeant First Class shared sage advice from his long career in the Infantry. He was the senior trainer at the Infantry Officer Basic Course, tasked with imparting leadership and combat wisdom to the Army's freshest crop of Lieutenants. We, being that group of new Lieutenants, knew almost nothing about life in the Army and hung on his every word.

The experienced trainer talked about foot marching, *"Listen, men ... you're gonna walk a lot of miles during your career as a grunt. And it's time to start toughening up your feet."* He relayed his methods for ensuring his feet could take him as far as he needed to go:

> "Wear your boots as often as possible ... I wear my combat boots out to dinner with my wife. You can put on foot powder before a march, if you want. I don't. And I don't wear socks because I want those calluses to stay tough, like leather."

We followed his advice ... and we got blisters.

Don't Be a Hard Ranger

Traditional military advice, and the recommendation from our seasoned platoon trainer, says to make the foot tougher than whatever it's rubbing against (sock liner, boot, etc.). It turns out that this "Hard Feet" approach to foot marching is exactly opposite of what distance hikers and ultra runners do to protect their feet.

Blisters come from the combination of friction, heat, and moisture. Foot powder and fresh socks can reduce moisture, but friction is unavoidable. And no amount of lace-tightening can prevent the foot from sliding forward and back with every step. So, it's a bit naive to expect skin to outlast the hostile environment inside the infantryman's boot over tens of thousands of steps.

The Foot Care Bible

At this point I must recommend a book that radically changed my approach to foot care, *Fixing Your Feet: Prevention and Treatments for Athletes* by Jon Vonhof. I read it while training for a long distance marching event years ago, which I survived blister free.

Vonhof has spent decades treating feet in the long distance racing community and covers everything from shoe sizing to toenail care to emergency treatments in the face of shredded feet. If foot care is at all part of your mission, buy his book now.

The Secret? ... Go Soft

Following the advice in *Fixing Your Feet*, then experimenting with my own preferences, here is my formula for making sure every foot march is blister-free.

- **Get rid of the calluses.** The "hard feet" theory is risky because over long movements, blisters can still form *under the calluses*. The friction damage occurs below the outer layers of toughened skin and results in excruciating pain. Prevent this calamity by using a pumice stone to file down the tough skin on all parts of your feet. Make the heel and balls of the feet just as smooth as the arch. This process will take weeks, so be patient.
- **Baby your feet.** After each pumice treatment, it's time to moisturize your feet. I use Miracle of Aloe Foot Repair Cream and it works wonders. Lotion will help keep your feet hydrated and pliable and will aid recovery after long marching hours. You can also soak your feet in Epsom salts following workouts, which will speed

recovery. If you can get past the flak your friends will give you, go get a pedicure. It'll be well worth it.

- **Trim the talons.** One overlooked step in preventing foot problems is toenail care. You should trim your toenails regularly and use a file on all rough surfaces. This will prevent the nail from snagging the sock and creating a bur that leads to pinpoint friction and a blister.

- **Apply skin lubricant.** This is the most radical departure from conventional military foot care "wisdom" and the most important step to this approach. Buy a stick of BodyGlide at any sports store or online and apply it directly to your feet prior to long walks. Endurance athletes typically use BodyGlide to lubricate and protect the thighs, groin, underarms, and occasionally the nipples. It lasts for hours and all but eliminates the friction problem inside the boot.

- **Find the right gear.** Your choice of equipment is decisive, so put the time into testing different combinations of boots, socks, laces, and liners. I went through four types of boots before settling on what I think are the most reliable and comfortable boots available, Blackhawk Warrior Wear Desert Ops Boots. I tried different types of laces (thick, thin, flat vs. tubular), as well as various lacing patterns (which Vonhof discusses). Then I experimented with no less than seven sock brands, finally settling on the Under Armour HeatGear Boot Sock. And just one pair at a time, although I tried two pairs at a time. I also tried sock liners but didn't prefer them.

So, my routine looks like this:

1. Trim and file the toenails.
2. File down the calluses.
3. Moisturize the feet one hour prior to walking.
4. Liberally apply BodyGlide 15 minutes before stepping off.
5. Don one pair of Under Armour socks inside of Blackhawk boots with the original Blackhawk laces tightened to comfort.
6. Walk a long way.
7. Soak the feet in Epsom salt for 15 minutes immediately afterwards.
8. Shower, then file the calluses again with a pumice stone.
9. Moisturize once more and relax with feet elevated.

What I've mentioned here is really just the beginning. To fully prepare yourself for hard days on your feet, I recommend becoming familiar with how to properly treat foot problems if they arise, as well as nutrition and training considerations. *Fixing Your Feet* is a great way to start.

Four Running Form Changes to Increase Speed and Efficiency

We do a lot of running in the military. But for as many miles as we log, we don't do much training on how to improve running form to get faster or prevent injury. The common thought is that running form is individual and unchangeable, and some people are just faster than others.

The civilian running community, however, has mountains of research-based advice showing that a few simple running form changes will:

- Improve your efficiency
- Increase your speed
- Extend your endurance
- Reduce injuries

Here is what I've found that works.

Shorten Your Stride Length

The first and most important change is to shorten your stride length. You are more efficient if you run with MORE steps rather than with LONGER steps. Long, slow strides have a great energy cost. You should strive to strike your right foot 90 times per minute. You can easily measure this by counting your steps over a 15 second interval and multiplying by 4. Using this method, you should be striking around 22 times every 15 seconds.

Shift to Midfoot Striking

When you reduce your stride length, you automatically begin to land more forward on your foot. This consequence is a great stress reliever for your heels, which are not designed to absorb shock. It is much better to land on the balls of your feet and use your calf muscles to land, rather than your heels and joints. It may feel like you are taking "baby steps," but you are saving your body unwanted stress.

Reduce Vertical Oscillation

Another positive result of a shorter stride is the reduction of vertical oscillation, or bounce. Bouncing up and down with each step indicates that you are directing your energy upward and not forward. Example: Suppose you were required to jump up and down 3,000 times, but you had the choice of jumping to a height of 3 inches or to a height of 1 inch, which would you choose? One inch, of course. It takes less energy and you would have to work less in order to achieve the shorter height. The same is true with running. You will take roughly 3,000 steps during a 4-mile run, so minimizing vertical bounce over that extended period of time will save energy in your stride and stress on your knees.

Minimize Support Time

Finally, you should also try to minimize your "support time" (or, the time your foot spends on the ground) by lifting your feet up quickly. Look at it this way, the longer your foot stays in the support position, the more of your potential energy is dissipated into the ground.

Consider this analogy: If you drop a tennis ball and a golf ball from the same height, which will bounce higher? The golf ball, because it is harder; it compresses less as it contacts the ground. However, the tennis ball flattens slightly when it hits the ground, losing a portion of its stored energy. Essentially, it stays on the ground longer than the golf ball and has less rebound power as a result. The process is the same with your feet. The longer you leave your foot on the ground, the more energy you transfer out of your stride that could be used to propel you forward.

Changing your running form should be a gradual and deliberate process. Schedule runs that are dedicated to experimenting with your form. Forget about speed and focus on finding the adjusted stride that works for you. You can also visit a specialized running store that will video your stride and provide valuable feedback.

Many of the above notes and examples came from *The Triathlete's Training Bible* by Joe Friel.

I Admit It ... I Forgot How to Workout

Try to remember the last hard physical day you've had. Perhaps you were exhausted, tested beyond your comfort zone, forced to give more than you thought was possible. Maybe it was Basic Training, or a unit obstacle course, or during a short-lived flirt with CrossFit. How long ago was it? Weeks? Months? Years?

The combat arms schools leaders go through are designed test students with exhaustive rites of passage to see if, somewhere down inside, they have what it takes to survive the battlefield. Leaders go through trials, then as we become more senior, we have the flexibility to avoid them. There are fewer and fewer people in a position to challenge us. The responsibility for pushing the limits shifts to the individual and what happens is that capability typically diminishes. We don't continue the test and we get soft.

That's what happened to me.

A Slow Leak

My physical fitness failure wasn't in volume, it was in diversity. As I moved out of my company command years and into the staff purgatory that are the Major years, the office became my place of duty and the demands on my time tripled. Instead of taking two hour mornings for PT and setting my own daily schedule, I found that meetings bookended my workouts, which were getting shorter and shorter. With less flexibility, I defaulted to my comfort zone, running and push-ups.

And for a combat leader, simply running and doing push-ups is lazy.

Goodbye Comfort Zone

It happened that a couple of years ago my wife bought a DVD workout program. At some point in the midst of babies and multiple moves to various duty stations, it got buried in a drawer and forgotten. Then one recent Saturday afternoon, I broke it out of the box and got started on a session, thinking I would sail through with ease. *"How hard could it be?"*

40 minutes later I was panting and sweating on my office floor, reduced to a withering pile of lactic acid. The video workout was full of high knees, squat jumps, lunges, kicking, and punching. It demanded explosive power, agility, balance, coordination, and ... oh yeah, heart. I had only completed *one* of the 20 workouts in this series lasting six weeks, but that's all it took for me to admit that I hadn't been challenging myself like I should've.

After a couple of weeks of regular sessions, the results appeared. I felt noticeably more *capable* and physically responsive. My legs felt more powerful, I had greater flexibility, and I was able to complete the exercises with less effort—all of which were effects that my running routine had not been producing.

Lead ... and Workout ... by Example

Physical fitness is a requirement for military service. *Combat-ready* physical fitness is different. It requires bursts of energy, heavy lifting, aerobic endurance, hand-eye coordination, fueling on the move, and an attitude that one must be ready for any test. The "finish line" in combat is a fluid concept. Selection never stops.

Those who will lead in combat must maintain their fitness capability because they set the standard for the team. Soldiers look to them for inspiration and ideas. Leaders should model both the discipline to continually test themselves, as well as the ingenuity to train for all the physical components of combat.

Take Your Pick

Nowadays, there is really no excuse for not pushing yourself and your team in creatively taxing ways.

CrossFit, SealFit, and StrongSwiftDurable have hundreds of free (and not so free) workouts that will yank you out of your comfort zone. TRX allows you to workout in any environment. And if you want a little motivation while you get smoked, try any flavor of the Beachbody series, including Insanity, P90X, and ... wait for it ... the Brazil Butt Lift.

If you'd rather race your way to exhaustion, obstacle course races are becoming more and more popular. Slosh your way through a Tough Mudder, battle Gladiators in a Spartan Race, or team up for a multi-skilled endurance challenge run by special operations cadre at GoRuck.

And don't forget that you can get a killer workout *and* training for combat with your favorite flavor of combatives.

No matter which method you chose, it's time to get deliberate about staying outside of your fitness comfort zone. Get over your fear and assumptions about popular workout programs. **Find a program that tests your fitness in unimaginable ways because the battlefield that awaits will test you in unimaginable ways.** What's more, the people you lead will base their preparation for that battlefield on your effort.

So, make it count.

18 Ways to Mitigate Off-Duty Risk

How_much should leaders involve themselves in subordinate lives to prevent off-duty risk? Too much involvement, and resentment and mistrust develop. Too little involvement, and potentially destructive problems grow unnoticed. Leaders hold passionate opinions on all sides of the discussion, but it's a safe conclusion that this area is truly *the art of leadership*.

This section is all about *The How*, the methods that leaders on every side of the discussion can use to achieve their intent. Those methods range from the "hands-off" approach to draconian micromanagement. Regardless, the mindful leader will devote time, organizational energy, and cognitive space to figuring out how to engage his or her people in this critical area of leadership.

The Indirect Approach

These are methods for the "hands-off" leader. Maybe the organization's members are mature and rarely have issues or incidents. They are also for the leader who values the subordinate's privacy and individual responsibility above all else, even at the expense of incurring risk. The goal is to provide support without imposing guidance or restrictions, to show concern and a willingness to assist, but only at the subordinate's request.

- **Display the resources.** Research the assistance agencies and options available to the service members, and display them prominently in common areas. This is often required by regulation or law (i.e., sexual assault reporting, equal opportunity), but if the leader is not going to engage deeply in personal matters, it's important to provide as many resources as possible.

- **Provide an easy out.** Many units have successfully used a "Taxi Fund" to give Soldiers a way to get back to barracks if they've had too much alcohol to drive. Can your subordinates also call you for help? Have you made it clear that you'll drop everything to get them out of trouble? Or, have you assumed that there won't be any problems? Or worse, that they'll just handle it themselves? Give out your number and make it clear that their safety is more important than your comfort.
- **Accentuate the positive.** A subtle way to avoid the bad is to talk continually about the good. "*Other units may get DUIs, but not this one. We're better than that.*" Positive reinforcement gives followers a frame of reference to live by and turns responsible behavior into a self-fulfilling prophecy.

Direct Engagement

This is the middle ground between "hands-off" and "iron fist." Most of us engage our units in this region of influence, fluctuating back and forth as incidents occur or chains of command implement their guidance. The key difference here is that leaders have frank conversations with subordinates about risk. Without a conversation, you're a "hands-off" leader.

- **Have the conversation.** In this arena, leading by example is not enough. Subordinates aren't looking to you for how to behave on the weekend and they aren't going to initiate a conversation about their weekend plans and the inherent risks therein. Leaders must start the conversation and engage in respectful ways that show true concern for the team's safety and acknowledge the maturity of the individuals.
- **Explain the terrain.** Talk openly about problems the unit is experiencing, as well as the successes that leaders achieve in reducing risk. It's critical that team members know what terrain they're fighting on.
- **Lead through your leaders.** Young service members may more readily take advice from peers and immediate supervisors than from higher up the chain of command. If you are a leader, use the

leaders at echelons below you to communicate the message. Rank isn't the most powerful aspect of this discussion; if it were, then generals would be giving the weekend safety briefs.

- **Bring in the experts.** Invite professionals to teach and discuss methods that leaders can use to connect with Soldiers. Professional counselors, medical providers, law enforcement, financial advisors, and chaplains can be helpful.

- **Highlight courage and sacrifice.** It's tough to think about getting wasted on the weekend when the First Sergeant is recounting the heroics of the most recent Medal of Honor recipient. Talking frequently about the high duty and sacrifice of the profession inserts an attitude of responsibility into the formation, which leaves little room for apathy and immaturity.

- **Reward action.** I had a battalion commander who gave out achievement medals to Soldiers who took action to mitigate off-duty risk. One such Soldier forced his drunk buddy (by almost physical means) to hand over the car keys outside a bar. Another called his platoon sergeant when he saw poor decision-making in the works. The commander recognized them in public, sending a strong statement.

- **Draw insight from all levels.** Ask the successful leaders to share their engagement techniques across the formation. This gives them credibility in public and shows that it's "cool" to be thinking of ways to reduce risk.

- **Get personal.** I once heard a speaker discuss the indiscriminate malice of the 9/11 attackers, saying, "The men who flew those planes into the Towers didn't care who they were going to kill. If you and I were there that morning, we'd be dead. Doesn't that make it more personal?" The statement resonated with me one Saturday while responding to a DUI the unit had the night before. Drunk drivers demonstrate the same indiscriminate nature. They have made a willful decision to lethally threaten anyone who is on the road with them, which could be you and your family, or even their own family. For service members, there is the added violation of trust in that we serve to protect our Nation's citizens, not place them at risk. Most people don't think about that aspect.

- **Plan for the <u>worst</u> scenario, not just the most likely.** The typical culprits of off-duty incidents are driving while intoxicated, speeding, bar fights, and domestic violence. But a designated driver doesn't do any good if the drunk Soldier is too intoxicated to find his way out of a burning night club or defend against a back-alley mugging. I've seen Soldiers try to cross train tracks or walk home in the freezing weather, both unsuccessfully. Identify and discuss those unlikely situations with your people. Emphasize that just a few moments of planning can mitigate lethal risk when it materializes.

- **AAR.** We conduct After Action Reviews for training and the annual Christmas party. Why not for weekend activities? Have a Monday chat with your team to find out if their weekend plans ended up the way you discussed it on Friday. See if they got into any situations they would've handled differently. How could they have better mitigated existing risk or prepared for an unexpected event?

A Draconian Environment

Leaders on this end of the scale tend to believe that they are responsible for individual failures and try to control their subordinates' off-duty behavior. Units (and duty stations) with frequent serious incidents exert more control in an effort to protect the population. At some point, however, the control measures undermine trust and subordinates become personally divested from the command's efforts.

- **Group punishment.** *"Whenever a Soldier gets a DUI, the entire company will report the next morning for extra training."* I've implemented that guidance ... *implemented*, not created. It's not fun for anyone. Group punishment is a tenuous argument because no one in the command has the ability (or authority) to control the individual actions of every Soldier. The idea is that the team members will dislike the punishment enough to correct the problem from within. Hopefully they do so in a way that conforms to your intent.
- **Make it relevant.** If you do have to shell out group punishment, put a moment of thought into the process and make it relevant. In the above reference, I was able to narrow the reporting formation from company to platoon and we went for a "little" jog on Saturday morning. We departed post and ran around the country roads until arriving at the exact bar the Soldier was drinking at before he got his DUI. The platoon lined up shoulder

to shoulder and the Soldier had to walk down the line retraining the act of handing his car keys to his buddy. *"I'm too drunk to drive, can you get me back to post?"* ... *"Anytime, Smith." "I'm too drunk to drive, can you get me back to post?"* ... *"Sure, and you'd better call me next time!"* The exercise was profoundly effective and relevant to the infraction.

- **Backbrief and verify.** We have all asked our subordinates what they plan on doing over the weekend, but how many times have we followed up to verify? For the hands-on approach, consider making a late night phone call to that Soldier who said he'd be at a bar on Saturday night. Sure, he probably stopped at one beer before thinking about driving home. But maybe he didn't and got lost in the good time. Maybe hearing his leader's voice will snap him back into a frame of mind to make a smart decision.
- **Weekend patrolling.** I was a company commander in a brigade that restationed from Washington to Germany—all 4,000 Soldiers, families, and equipment. It was a fascinating social experiment to watch underage Soldiers displace to an environment where drinking was now legal. The serious incidents flourished, across all ranks, not just junior enlisted. The commander cracked down with a risk mitigation operation that put every officer and NCO leader out in the local towns in uniform to prevent incidents. It was painful for all, but it worked.
- **Sign on the dotted line.** In extreme situations, I've heard of leaders forming an agreement with their team members about risk activity, even to the point of signing a contract. It's demeaning and it's probably against regulation, but it's a method.

More Important than Policy

Whatever you choose to do, subordinates have to know you care. **Or more directly, you have to care about your people!** Approach the discussion from that standpoint, not from a position of policy and guidance. How would you help your own adult son or daughter mitigate this risk?

There is but one way to do more — honestly care about them.
Everything, yes, everything else is technique.
~ Colonel Ross Coffman

11 Keyboard Shortcuts You Must Learn

There are few obvious skills that military leaders need to be experts at. Digital efficiency is usually not cited as one of them. **But where do we spend the vast majority of our time?** Behind the computer. Why not focus some effort on learning ways to be more efficient there?

Here are a few basic keyboard shortcuts that you should already be using:

- **CTRL+C** – Copy the selected item/text
- **CTRL+X** – Cut the selected item/text
- **CTRL+V** – Paste the copied/cut item
- **CTRL+A** – Select all the items/text in a document

And here are 11 powerful shortcuts that could make you lethal behind the keyboard:

- **ALT+TAB** – Switch between open program windows. This shortcut is a must to quickly transition from Outlook to other programs.
- **CTRL+Mouse Click** – Select multiple items. (Remember: you must hold down the CTRL key until you are done selecting items.) Use this shortcut when making formatting changes to PowerPoint shapes/items. I once had a boss who would painstakingly click and format each shape one at a time. He had no idea that you could select multiple items at once to format them the same way. Very painful to work for!
- **CTRL+D** – Duplicate the selected item. This is very useful in PowerPoint, when you're building icons and making slides.
- **CTRL+Z** – Undo the last action.

- **CTRL+Y** – Redo the last action.
- **CTRL+left/right arrow** – Jump the cursor to the beginning of the next/previous word. Very handy when editing emails or text. Please don't waste time by holding down the arrow to move your cursor across the screen.
- **CTRL+up/down arrow** – Jump the cursor to the beginning of the next/previous paragraph.
- **CTRL+BACKSPACE** – Delete the entire previous word.
- **CTRL+DELETE** – Delete the entire upcoming word.
- **CTRL+Roll Mouse Ball** – zoom in/out in the selected window. Use this to size/resize the view on your slides or document. It will also work in Explorer to resize web pages.
- **CTRL+SHIFT+B** – Open the Outlook Address Book. This is quicker than moving the mouse to open your address book to search for a name.

17 Productivity Hacks for Your Military Staff

I bet that more than once a day, you let out a sigh of frustration at the absentminded staff activity that surrounds you: Your boss asks why you didn't respond to his "urgent" email. THE NEW OPERATIONS NCO TYPES IN ALL CAPS (incredibly annoying). Someone prints 30 full-page copies of the 53-slide presentation because, *there are 30 people in the meeting, right?"* And in that meeting, your unit's update doesn't make it to the slides, even though you sent them yesterday.

And those are just the ones you notice! There are probably dozens more inefficiencies, idiosyncrasies, and ineptitudes you aren't even aware of that impair you and your staff's productivity.

Having spent a few years in the Army staff machine, I offer these immediate adjustments to reclaim your sanity and reduce the needless, often well-intentioned but inefficient staff practices that keep you from getting more important work done.

Email

Let's start with email. We hate it, but it's the military's most prolific communication tool. We spend more time on email than anywhere else, yet we rarely issue guidance specifically aimed at becoming more efficient at managing it. If you have any authority over a group's activity on email, implement these changes right away:

- **Type in the BLUF.** (BLUF is Bottom Line Up Front, by the way) What military leader has time to go searching for the main point of an email? Commanders and key staff members certainly don't, and shouldn't have to scroll to find it. Start your emails with the bottom line and you will find that it forces you to specify your recommendation, it condenses your supporting writing, and people appreciate it greatly.

- **Maximize the signature block.** Have you ever needed to call someone and figured you'd just flip to one of their emails to get the number? ... and then slammed your mouse on the desk when you discovered no signature block? Those are some of my most annoyed moments at work. Fix the problem right away by creating a signature block template and making it mandatory for your people to use it. Put in all the unit mottos and life-changing quotes you want, but for goodness sakes put your phone/email contact information in there. And this is important: Set them to display on Forwards and Replies, not just New Email. It sounds nerdy, but people inside and outside your organization will silently thank you.

- **Set some rules.** Did you know that in Microsoft Outlook, you can set a rule to display your boss's emails in red font? Or that you can flag all emails about the upcoming deployment? Or that you can redirect the daily unit reports to a specific folder for browsing later? Spend a moment thinking about whose communication is priority, what information you need to know immediately, and what information you can pool into batches for consumption later. Then customize your inbox so you don't have to repeat the process for every new email. (Find the Rules Wizard under the "Home" tab in Outlook.)

- **Call instead.** If you've got an urgent item that needs attention, do not rely on email. Go face to face or make a phone call. You can't hold someone accountable for critical information if you use a passive communication method to transmit it.

- **Save the clicks.** If you're not using the Message Preview Pane, it's time to up your game. Put it on the right side of your Outlook window (not below your messages), so you can read a whole email without having to scroll. If you do have to scroll, use the spacebar instead of moving to the mouse.

- **Speaking of keyboard shortcuts.** CTRL+R replies to the current email. **CTRL+F** forwards it. **CTRL+N** creates a new message. **CTRL+SHIFT+B** brings up the address book. **CTRL+ENTER** sends your message (I love that one! So much quicker than transitioning to the mouse.)

Why am I talking about individual email practices in a post about staff productivity? Yes, so you become more efficient. But more importantly, so you can teach your team to become more efficient. The quicker they can perform routine tasks, the more they can accomplish.

- **Remove distractions.** Research shows that distractions at work turn us into cognitive 5th graders. The constant pings from our connected network pull us out of the creative mode and prevent us from contributing our best work. If you've got a big project to do, go silent. Set an Out of Office email reply or block off time on your calendar to focus. If you're really bold, then turn off email notifications all together and set "email hours" dedicated to burning through your inbox. To be safe, I do recommend you set active notifications for emails, texts, and calls from your boss.

- **Don't let others plan your day.** Another key productivity concept regarding email is that it's a horrible way to start your day. Read any number of several books on productivity and you'll see that people get more done when they set their own priorities and control the time allocated to accomplishing them. Email does the opposite. It opens up a window for everyone else to heap requirements on you, draws you into reactive mode, and increases stress. *"Please review these slides." "What's your guidance for next week's meeting agenda?" "The exercise shifted one week to the right."* And on and on … Sure, the information might be important, but only at the right time. Use the first moments or even hours of the morning to plan and prioritize your day, or perhaps complete creative work you're responsible for.

Ok, enough about email. On to the really exciting tips …

Printing

- **Just tell them what to print.** If you haven't given your people guidance about what and how much you want printed, you're destroying the planet! Ok, that's a little dramatic, but raise your hand if you've ever seen a leader sit through an entire meeting without touching the stack of slides in front of him. Or better yet, he comments on how he doesn't even need them or prefers two per page printouts.

Army staffs don't like to admit it, but print paper costs money. During the Sequestration Crisis of 2012, when we were deciding whether to buy toilet paper for the barracks or fuel for training, we basically stopped all printing in my regiment.

Although it sounds tedious and silly, leaders could save a lot of money and time by issuing guidance for print requirements. Decide which key leaders get printouts and tell them when to print one slide per page versus multiple. (A moment of introspection will reveal that there is typically no reason you can't print more than one slide per page.) Challenge your staff to use only digital copies, or at least print on the back of the page as well.

[**Pro tip:** Get the most out of your print area by using the printer settings instead of PowerPoint settings to set the print layout. Ever wondered how to print four slides per page with no margin? Here's how to do it: From the PowerPoint Print tab, go to Printer Properties and select 4 slides per page. Then back in the PowerPoint Print tab, select "Full Page Slides" and "Scale to Fit Paper." Those settings will give you four slides in Landscape mode that fill the entire print page.]

Meetings

- **Send read-ahead packets.** On a related topic, have you EVER been in a unit that actually sent read-ahead slides a day or two before a meeting? I have, once. It was a welcomed relief to the hurried frenzy that accompanied meetings in my other units. Yes, it is possible to send out read-ahead slides—leaders just have to accept that the information might be more than 24 hours old. But if you give an honest look, you'll find that very little information we brief in military units needs to be real time. I'm talking about Training Meetings, Command and Staff, USR, and even some operational briefs. Set the deadline for information requirements and give your people a chance to consolidate the data and make it presentable the day before (not minutes before) the brief. People will eventually get used to the earlier timeline. This method lets people print their own copies (if needed) and gives them a chance to see the train before it hits them in the meeting.

- **"Got a minute?"** Sometimes it feels like what takes up most of our time are the meetings that aren't on the calendar, when someone knocks on the door and asks, *"Got a minute?"* What they really mean is, *"Would you please stop what you're doing for an indefinite length of time to discuss a topic you're not prepared to talk about?"* Just like email notifications, drop-by chats can break your concentration and really veer your day off course. Instead of suffering through it, block off a portion of your day that's open for anyone to come by with their 5-minute issue. It could be an unstructured window of time or you can split up the time by unit or staff section (*"The S3 has 1545-1600. A Co. has 1600-1615."* And so on.) This method not only protects your productivity but gives subordinates time that they know is theirs and will prepare for.

- **Pin the rose.** A task or request for information is destined to incompletion without a point of contact and a due date. When you identify actions that must occur, pin the rose on someone right away, set a timeline for completion, and review them at the end of the meeting. And you can track those tasks using any number of tools – Microsoft Tasks, SharePoint Tasks, or even just the whiteboard.

Quick Fixes

Here are a few one-off tips to consider in making your work life a little more efficient and a little less frustrating.

- **Product standardization.** If your section, unit, or staff publishes something, it should be standardized. That goes for slides, operations orders, memos, letters, and even internal communication. Templates set an expectation baseline, make it easier to spot mistakes, and provide predictability for subordinate HQs.

- **Turn off the TV.** Unless you work at a strategic level office that has to respond to world events, you don't need 24/7 news. It's a distraction and it's a depressant. If you prefer some type of background noise, go for music instead.

- **Set reminders.** It takes 5 seconds to tell Siri to remind you to do your Cyber Awareness training, or to send the weekly update to the boss, or to check on a subordinate who lost a family member last week. Use the digital tools available to enhance your work activity.

- **Go old school.** Print and carry a hard copy of key phone numbers and email addresses. It will come in handy when your 3-year-old drops your phone in the toilet.

The Golden Staff Rule

Finally, it's time to stop what is perhaps the biggest cause of staff inefficiency: **creating more questions instead of providing answers.**

Higher headquarters staffs frustrate subordinate units when they publish cursory products and give vague guidance. Writing in passive voice is often a problem (*"Ammunition will be delivered to A Co. at 0700."* Great, but by whom???). So is the tendency for staff members to receive taskings and simply copy/paste them to lower headquarters for execution.

When higher level staff doesn't do its homework on what it will take to execute its own guidance, lower level staffs must respond with basic coordination questions. With multiple lower units demanding clarification, higher staff gets bogged down answering everyone and must amend the guidance.

Before publishing that order or issuing guidance, ask yourself and your staff:

- Could the reader complete the mission based on this guidance and nothing else?

- Have we assigned responsibility and POC information for every action and element involved?
- If we received this guidance from our higher headquarters, could we execute it?
- What factors will the subordinate units have to consider in executing this guidance and can we make it clear where this fits into other priorities?

What Combat Leaders Need to Know About Neuroscience

We remember the books that change us—that alter our thinking, move us emotionally, or reveal unseen, enlightening perspectives. Powell's *My American Journey* did that for me. So did Bill Bryson's *A Short History of Nearly Everything*. And when I read Malcolm Gladwell's *Blink* in 2007, I recall connecting so many new insights that I didn't have enough book margins to capture them all. The relevancy for the military profession spilled off of the pages and sparked an intellectual curiosity that has lasted for years.

The topic is neuroscience and the breakthrough discoveries that its researchers have made in recent years. Neuroscientists publish fascinating scientific papers about how the brain functions. Authors like Gladwell, Jonah Lehrer, David Rock, Joseph LeDoux, and others translate this technical work into digestible language with real world application. From decision psychology to organizational efficiency to change detection and management, new understanding of the brain is changing how we live our lives.

But as I made connections from neuroscience to the military profession, specifically tactical combat leadership, I found few resources to aid the service member, Dave Grossman's *On Killing* and *Warrior Mindset* being the most useful. So I decided to embark on a personal quest to publish *something* that references neuroscience to improve military leader performance. What resulted was my first published article and a Master's thesis on the topic. This section is an adapted version of that endeavor.

*"Everything you do in life is based on your brain's
determination to minimize danger or maximize reward."*[1]

The brain wants to move toward things in life that give it pleasure or ensure survival, and away from things that cause pain or threaten survival.[2] Combat demands that military individuals overcome this natural impulse to survive and move toward the danger. From this perspective, **succeeding in combat is a measure of how well the brain copes with dangerous situations and performs tasks that ensure survival.**

The field of neuroscience has seen significant advances in recent years, and the benefits of this knowledge can positively affect numerous disciplines, including combat leadership. Using functional Magnetic Resonance Imaging (*f*MRI), surgical methods, and experiment-based approaches, researchers have revealed many of the biological processes that underlie our most basic emotional and cognitive behaviors, such as how and why we react to threatening situations, how our brains allocate energy to cope with competing demands, and how our senses interact with our minds to create the world we know.[3]

Learning about brain function and physical reactions to stress does not simply inform the leader, but creates self-awareness that makes him better able to control those processes.[4] Tactical-level military leaders can use this new knowledge to understand the effects of combat, anticipate and recognize cognitive reactions, and adjust their leadership abilities to succeed in difficult situations. They can do this by performing exercises to decrease physiological stress reactions, using emotionally-controlled leadership to guide their organizations, and creating an environment during battle that facilitates effective decision making. By educating Soldiers about brain function and incorporating cognitive stressors into training, leaders can prepare their units to perform in battle with emotional stability.

Brain Basics

Combat leaders need a basic knowledge of cerebral biology to understand the importance of the mind's function during combat. The two major brain areas most relevant to this topic are the limbic system and the prefrontal cortex.[5] The former is the collection of brain regions involved in emotions, learning, and memory. The latter is the center for higher-level thinking, which actively influences body functions and performance.[6] Inputs travel along pathways in both of these systems and allow us to react to scenarios with a balance of emotion and reason.

Located in the center of the brain, the limbic system primarily contains the thalamus, hypothalamus, hippocampus, and the amygdala, and is the creator of emotions and memory.[7] Its primary function is to interpret information sent from the body's senses and to issue emotional commands back to the body. The limbic system also sends its data to the executive areas of the brain (frontal lobe) for cognitive processing and receives instructions about how the body should respond to the given situation.[8]

Sometimes, the limbic system can independently respond to the world, like when we react to threatening situations. This occurs at the subconscious level, when the amygdala—the fear and anxiety response center— compares data from the world with the hippocampus, which is the memory database of experiences.[9] If the incoming information corresponds to a threat that has been tagged as negative or dangerous, the amygdala immediately commands the body into action. We have all experienced this process when our reflexes have caused us to snatch a hand away from a closing door or leap away from a snake.[10]

The more sophisticated processes of the mind occur in a sheet of tissue just behind the forehead known as the prefrontal cortex. As explained by Dr. Rand Swenson of Dartmouth Medical School, the prefrontal cortex is also known as the "thinking brain," the manager of "memory, judgment, planning, sequencing of activity, abstract reasoning, impulse control, personality, reactivity to the surroundings, and mood."[11] This area is what allows humans to solve math problems, develop abstract concepts, and ponder our own existence. **It is also the area that military leaders use to balance risks in combat, develop courses of action, and create strategies to lead effectively.**

Every part of the brain is packed with blood vessels that provide the oxygen needed to fuel its 100 billion cells.[12] As we engage various brain systems during daily activity (e.g., driving, throwing a ball), the brain redirects blood and glucose to the appropriate areas (e.g. visual cortex, motor cortex) to fuel the most important event occurring at the time.[13] This allocation leaves less fuel for other brain functions, like cognitive control, which requires vast amounts of blood and glucose to operate.[14]

When the limbic system is heavily engaged, as it is during the high threat stress of combat, it will quite literally steal fuel from the prefrontal cortex, thus handicapping a leader's ability to combat the situation with cognition. [15] As successful business consultant and CEO David Rock explains in *Your Brain at Work,* "the degree of activation of the limbic system is the *degree of deactivation* [emphasis added] of the prefrontal cortex."[16] Brain research has also shown that there are many more neural connections that flow from the amygdala directly to the prefrontal cortex than vice versa. [17] Therefore, it is easy for our emotions to guide or suppress our rational thoughts. This is a crucial vulnerability because military leaders must preserve cognitive function when leading during combat.

The Limbic System in Combat

The limbic system is evolutionarily older than the prefrontal cortex—primitively old, in fact. It developed to help man survive the ancient battlefield of predator versus prey. The limbic system has the "chemical authority" to initiate rapid responses to threats and is good at doing so.[18] The amygdala ignites; adrenaline flows to the blood; the pulse races; the eyes focus and rapidly scan for a threatening movement.[19] We halt unnecessary digestion and tense major muscle groups in preparation for a clash. Then the brain, teeming with blood vessels, redirects the available supply of oxygen and glucose-rich blood to the limbic and motor areas so that we can react quickly in the impending fight.

At this point, the mind is in its most basic survival mode; it has no spare energy to devote to solving geometry problems or to pondering philosophical dilemmas. This biological decision to focus resources toward limbic areas during dangerous situations is what keeps us alive at a time when a cerebral problem-solving approach would be fatally slow.

But today's military leaders do not face the same world that our ancestors did. While there are still many threats that require rapid, reflexive action, leaders also have to manage countless streams of information; communicate over multiple technological systems; balance political, military, and civilian considerations; and lead hundreds of men and women in the process. **Combat requires a coherent and rational mind.**

Combat is full of stressful moments—initial contact with the enemy, rushing to secure enemy terrain, or responding to an unexpected event— that test emotional resolve. Those involved experience intense sensory input and encounter debilitating explosions, grotesque scenes, and threatening enemy movements. As the limbic system attempts to keep pace with the environment, it starves the soldier's ability to maintain a clear mental framework. Coupled with the typically exhausting physical exertion of combat, **Soldiers are consistently at risk of degraded cognitive processing.**

This occurrence is evident in countless historical accounts of Soldiers rendered immobile by battle. In his survey of soldier actions in World War II, the famous soldier author S.L.A. Marshall observed: "Some fail to act mainly because they are puzzled what to do and their leaders do not tell them; others are wholly unnerved and can neither think nor move in sensible relation to the situation."[20]

Renowned historian J.F.C. Fuller's observation is similar: "In an attack half of the men on a firing line are in terror and the other half are unnerved."[21] Works by Bruce Siddel and Dave Grossman, particularly *Sharpening the Warrior's Edge* and *On Combat*, present an exhaustive analysis of combat's effect on the human body and what Soldiers can expect when they face it.[22]

The Leader in Combat

Each duty position on the battlefield contains some balance of reflexive and cognitive tasks. Some can be trained repeatedly and developed into muscle memory, like loading and firing a weapon. Others are more cognitive in nature, like calling for indirect fire or coordinating a synchronized attack. While each soldier has his own personal tactical situation to react to, typically frontline riflemen operate in the reflexive region, while the cognitive component of battle increases with rank and responsibility.

For this section, the term "leader" refers to any individual who is responsible for leading several groups of Soldiers in maneuver against the enemy and must manage multiple battlefield systems. This leader spends most of his battlefield time outside of his weapon's sights. While team and squad leaders are unquestionably "leaders," they use battle drills and reflexive training to guide most of their actions and will not have to rely on their abstract cognitive abilities during combat unless they are operating as an autonomous element.

The platoon leader and platoon sergeant are the first leaders who engage in more complex problem solving than direct-fire battle. The company-level commander is squarely in the cognitive region, with occasional moments that require reflexive action. The battalion-level commander will rarely perform actions that are not based on premeditated cognition.

What can these leaders do to mitigate the physical reactions to stress that will inevitably occur? What methods are available to regain cognitive control and place the leader in a position to maximally benefit the unit? First, actively decrease the effects of stress. Second, infuse emotional stability into the organization. Finally, create an environment that facilitates effective decision making.

Control the effect of emotional energy

"While many animals get through life mostly on emotional automatic pilot, those animals that can readily switch from automatic pilot to willful control have a tremendous advantage."[23]

As combat will readily reveal, the body and mind undergo rapid changes when reacting to stress. While moderate levels of stress improve functions like motor skills, stress can easily impair performance in cognitive areas, where today's tactical leaders typically need to operate.[24] Heart rate, blood pressure, and breathing will all increase; digestion will slow and nausea may occur; speech may falter, and auditory and visual cues may diminish.[25] All of these effects are natural as the body emotionally reacts to the fight. However, **leaders have a responsibility to control the effect of emotional energy and remain calm in the face of danger.**

One proven technique used by law enforcement and military professionals to combat stress is tactical breathing.[26] As Grossman explains, tactical breathing is "a tool to control the sympathetic nervous system" that will "slow your thumping heart, reduce the tremble in your hands, deepen your voice" and "bathe yourself with a powerful sense of calm and control."[27] As one of the only two autonomic nervous system actions that we can control (the other is blinking), breath rate is the first reaction to stress that leaders can rein in.[28]

Immediately after a significant stressor occurs (e.g., the enemy initiates contact) or just prior to entering a high-stress situation (e.g., the final approach to an objective), simply take several successive deep breaths and hold each one for three to five seconds. As you breathe, visualize your body relaxing and remaining calm during the event. Although time may not allow leaders to take a long tactical pause, simply diagnosing a rapid breathing pattern and forcing a couple of slow breaths will help decrease the body's agitated state.

Another method of controlling stress is a concept called *labeling and reappraisal,* which is the act of naming the emotional state you are experiencing and actively reassigning a new emotion that is more productive for the situation.[29] Verbally identifying the emotions or reassuring yourself out loud activates the prefrontal cortex and begins to reclaim some power from the limbic system.[30]

Simple cue-words like "steady," "stay focused," and "relax," are active reminders that can elicit controlled behavior. A unit's motto can be another steadying phrase. Repeating these words can trigger confidence and strength in the face of trying circumstances. More importantly, such statements not only have an effect on leaders, but can also filter through an organization to reinforce its members. The key is to talk oneself into a mental framework that is capable of handling the highly cognitive experience of modern combat.

Any military leader will readily support the practice of unit rehearsals before an operation. **Do individuals not also have the responsibility to rehearse how they will react in combat?** Professional golfers, divers, and other elites who rely on precise skills use a technique called visualization to reinforce desired behavior. Likewise, a tactical leader can benefit by visualizing himself performing with emotional calm and cognitive clarity. A leader with a clear vision of how he wants to perform will, as survival author Laurence Gonzales puts it, create a kind of "memory of the future" that the brain can access during combat.[31] Like muscle memory, proper mental processes can become reflexive.

Infuse emotional stability and control into the organization

Leaders must discover ways to control their application of emotional energy. Their behavior is a compass for the unit, an indicator of what stress is allowable and appropriate for the situation. The first actions after a significant event—like an attack by an improvised explosive device—set the unit's tone for the engagement. As General George S. Patton counseled, leaders are always on parade.[32] An uncontrolled yell, a high-pitched radio call, or even a worrisome look can transmit stress and doubt to the unit. Conversely, leaders with composure and confidence despite stressful circumstances will infuse those traits into the unit. Commanders should be deliberate and concise. Leaders should objectively verify emerging information to avoid overreacting or acting too hastily.

Neuroscience research reveals that there are methods leaders can use to do this. Noted author Malcolm Gladwell describes "deliberate emotion" in *Blink*:

> We take it as a given that first we experience an emotion, and then we may—or may not—express that emotion in our face. We think of the face as the residue of emotion. The process works in the opposite direction as well. Emotion can also start in the face. It is an equal partner in the emotional process.[33]

A German psychology experiment revealed that people who were physically made to smile by holding a pen clenched in their teeth rated cartoons as funnier than people who watched the same cartoons while holding a pen in their lips, which prevented smiling.[34] Facial expressions are not just a representation of emotions, they can *direct* emotions. Leaders can physically incite a more positive, relaxed emotional response in their bodies by intentionally forming a relaxed facial expression during combat events. This demeanor will also cue similar responses in the Soldiers around them.

Create an effective decision making environment

"Insight comes from a quiet brain."[35]

Regardless of rank, and even in the midst of intense combat, **leaders must create an environment that is conducive to making cognitive, not emotional, decisions.** They can start creating this environment by physically and emotionally disengaging from the immediate fight. This may mean finding sufficient cover for a local command post. A company commander seldom belongs in the hatch of his vehicle or exposed on a street scanning for targets like a rifleman. Of course, desperate times will call for every gun to be in the fight, but only a handful of commanders will ever face that situation.

The goal is for the leader to mentally "zoom out" from his personal tactical situation and take a more macro-level view of the battle, preparing his brain to handle the impending cognitive challenges. Get out of the weapon sights and into cover, where you can actually think.

The commander should then use his "space" from the battle to focus on what he has trained to do: Assess and analyze what has occurred, recognize friendly force vulnerabilities, predict what the enemy will do next, decide on a feasible course of action, communicate the plan to the unit, and apply the appropriate leadership skills to inspire the unit to accomplish the mission.

The specifics of these steps can include conducting rapid terrain analysis and land navigation using complex digital systems; calling for mortar, artillery, or aircraft fires; establishing hasty graphic control measures to prevent fratricide; assimilating frantic, vague reports from subordinates; and relaying relevant data to higher echelons, among many other tasks. **These are not reflexive actions that one can repeat until they are muscle memory,** nor are they actions that the emotional limbic system can control. They are highly cognitive and require a steady mind.

A leader needs to find a suitable environment where she or he can generate new ideas, new insights, for each unique tactical situation encountered. Battle drills are, of course, an effective method units use to survive the first moments of a new event. **But leaders must think beyond the battle drill and formulate innovative ways to beat the enemy.** As neuroscientist Jonah Lehrer explains in *How We Decide*, "This is where the prefrontal cortex really demonstrates its unique strengths. It is the only brain region able to take an abstract principle and apply it in an unfamiliar context to come up with an entirely original solution."[36]

The brain assembles new ideas using a system called "working memory." Working memory is the temporary storage area the prefrontal cortex uses to hold concepts in place while it accesses other, more permanent bits of information (like stored knowledge, past experiences, and technical data). [37] This ability "allows the brain to make creative associations as seemingly unrelated sensations and ideas overlap."[38] "Once this overlapping of ideas occurs, cortical cells start to form connections that have never existed before, wiring themselves into entirely new networks."[39]

To create new ideas in combat, leaders must enable and facilitate this process. They must "think about what they're thinking about." The prefrontal cortex cannot generate new ideas while stressful events constantly bombard its working memory. Leaders must protect their cognitive faculties, prioritize facts, and not let extraneous information distract them.[40] Sometimes deliberate problem solving is necessary; other situations are novel and require a creative solution.

When successful, the prefrontal cortex will hold the crucial facts of the situation in its working memory and compare them with previous knowledge and experience to generate new solutions. Again, this can only occur when the leader has created a suitable environment. He will not obtain any genuine insights if he is distracted by incoming fire, annoyed by a radio operator screaming information, or if he has allowed his stress levels to spike.

In combat, the process may occur like this: The enemy attacks on one side of a platoon combat outpost with machine gun and rocket fire. The platoon's guard force reacts instinctively, returning fire where possible, but the platoon sergeant breaks his gaze from the explosions and asks, "What else can be happening here?" When he disengages his working memory from the visually overloading stimulus and thus momentarily quiets his brain, his mind begins to process the events in light of other stored knowledge, such as a report of a previous attack in which the enemy used gunfire and rockets as a diversion to support a larger attack from the opposite direction. With the insight that this first attack could be a diversion, the platoon sergeant informs the unit and wargames with the platoon leader where a second attack might occur. **Such insight will not happen if leaders are myopically focused on the near fight to the extent that it prevents their cognitive abilities from engaging.**

Once a leader achieves a state of comparative emotional calm, he permits his mind to sense patterns in the environment that otherwise might have been suppressed by stress or distraction. Neuroscience research explains what we all have sensed at one time or another—that the mind can know something about our surroundings before we are fully aware of it.

Detecting subtle patterns is the job of a group of brain regions called the basal ganglia, which have connections to virtually every part of the brain. [41] The basal ganglia subconsciously process massive amounts of data and send signals that cause visceral, emotional responses to the body.[42] This is what happens when you walk out the door without your car keys and have a gut feeling that "I'm forgetting something …"

A leader can access this process during combat, but only if he is tuned in to listen for it. The brain can analyze the developing situation and compare the data with the lifetime of knowledge, experience, doctrine, and lessons that have accumulated in long-term memory. It will filter out extraneous information, discover relevant patterns of information, and, using emotions, alert the body that the prefrontal cortex should redirect its attention.[43] In this way, hunches are not just superfluous feelings, but expressions of powerful analytical processes hard at work.

A Model for Cognitive Battle

In *Your Brain at Work*, David Rock explains that the mental processes relevant to performing work are *understanding, recalling, deciding, memorizing,* and *inhibiting.*[44] His example involves a business leader who must complete a proposal by focusing on relevant information, remembering similar past proposals, selecting the best method to complete the proposal, committing applicable information to long-term memory, and blocking out mental processes not beneficial for the task. Military leaders must perform similar cognitive tasks when responding to a combat situation. The difficulty of their task is compounded because every battlefield is different, and every battlefield is deadly. Let's examine a typical combat engagement.

Understanding. Following the initial shock of an attack, understanding involves how a leader "creates maps in the prefrontal cortex that represent new, incoming information and connects these maps to existing maps in the rest of the brain."[45] It means absorbing the relevant terrain (which is unanticipated terrain if the enemy initiated the attack) and overlaying it with pertinent data like population considerations, maneuverability requirements and restrictions, and friendly force disposition. The leader accepts and adjusts to his new environment as the arena in which he will fight, and then begins to form his new mental map. This is also the opportunity to sense patterns in the environment that may affect the decisions to come.

Recalling. In battle, recalling is the process of comparing the existing situation with the database of stored knowledge in the long-term memory networks. Think of it as looking into the cupboard to identify what ingredients are available to make dinner. This important mental process filters through all lessons, instruction, and experiences to determine what can be used to cope with the current situation. While being attacked from a building, for instance, the leader's mind may instantly make connections to the doctrine he learned in his early years. Then, the lessons learned from dozens of urban exercises reestablish their neural link to the prefrontal cortex and make themselves available for use. Maybe a phrase or piece of advice from a former instructor just pops into his head. Recalling is the brain's way of gathering the most relevant information in anticipation of making a complex decision.

Deciding. A combat leader's brain engages in the deciding process when it chooses which recalled information will be most useful and applies it to the real-time world to build a new mental map. **This is cognitive course of action**

development. Deciding brings together learned skills and past knowledge to form a response plan specific to the current scenario. Sometimes a leader firmly decides on a course of action; other times, the cumulative effect of the recalling process creates emotional hunches that point to a certain response. After deciding on a course of action, the brain shifts from conceptual analysis to specific application. The new mental map now occupies the working memory space and the prefrontal cortex engages to find detailed answers needed for execution. These include what route friendly forces will take, when and where they will engage, what fire control measures subordinate units need, what information must be passed higher, and so on.

Memorizing. David Rock describes memorizing as "holding maps in attention in the prefrontal cortex long enough to embed them in long-term memory."[46] Research shows that it is impossible for our brains to simultaneously hold multiple complex concepts in working memory without degrading accuracy.[47] (Imagine trying to type a text message while driving in England on the left side of the road.) In combat, rapidly comparing the details of multiple courses of action is quite a difficult task. Thus, it is important for leaders to move the mental map of a battle plan into long-term memory so the prefrontal cortex can reoccupy working memory. This allows the comparison of the plan with new ideas and emerging information.

For leaders in battle, memorizing is also the internalization of a plan. Focusing on the concept of an operation (planned or hasty) creates familiarity that allows execution without redundant analysis or reference to written notes. Memorizing is a form of rehearsal and wargaming for leaders, compelling them to review their plan from multiple angles and search for vulnerabilities or errors.

Inhibiting. Finally, inhibiting is the practice of selective focus, when one actively tries to not engage certain mental maps because they are irrelevant or counterproductive.[48] An American driver in England should actively try to forget the mental perspective of driving on the right-hand side of the road. Working memory cannot juggle two competing complex concepts without diminished efficiency. As a combat example, consider a leader who has only Iraq deployment experience and was almost entirely engaged with IEDs. She spent the year concentrating on how to defeat IEDs and focused battle drills to respond accordingly. Now in Afghanistan, where the enemy in her particular region conducts exclusively small-arms and rocket attacks, the leader must suppress her learned tendencies, realign her mental perspective, and develop new neural connections that will help her properly frame and respond to the most likely threat.

Personalizing. To these, I add personalizing, which can apply to every moment of a leader's day. This is the application of leadership principles and personality attributes that will guide the organization to accomplish the mission effectively. There are many examples of leaders who, intentionally or not, seem to change their personality in combat. The emotional stress of the situation causes them to display different leadership traits than they demonstrated in training. Personalizing is the leader's conscious effort to prevent external influences from altering the foundation of character and leadership that he has consistently developed and that her subordinates have learned to expect.

How to Train for the Emotionally Stable Fight

> *"It therefore follows that the far object of a training system is to prepare the combat officer mentally so that he can cope with the unusual and the unexpected as if it were the altogether normal and give him poise in a situation where all else is in disequilibrium."*[49]

Training for combat is about changing the brain. Decades of neuroscience research have firmly shown that the brain is highly adaptable and that repeated activities designed to create specific behaviors—like combat training—literally "change cellular structure and strength of connections between neurons."[50] At the rifleman level, training teaches Soldiers to respond reflexively to situations that demand a spontaneous conditioned response, such as engaging an enemy fighter at close range. It is the same behavioral process that professional athletes apply to develop the fine-tuned motor skills needed in competition.

This learning process also applies to activities that demand higher cognitive ability, such as detailed planning for a combat operation or reacting to a complex attack. A way to train this capability would be to construct an exercise that requires leaders to undergo physical or fear-induced stress and then perform deliberate, time-constrained planning for an ambiguous situation.[51] This could be a simple puzzle-solving activity or a complicated vignette-based planning exercise that incorporates combat systems. This "cognitive stress shoot" would allow leaders to discover their personal responses to stress and identify useful techniques to overcome the cognitive disabilities associated with stressful events.[52]

Units should also structure training to present multiple streams of information and detectable patterns of enemy activity that will teach leaders what to look for. Historical battle accounts reveal that small changes in the environment, like a lack of regular street activity, can sound subconscious alarms. Constructing patterns in training and then altering them can teach leaders to listen to their hunches and be extra vigilant when "something doesn't feel right." Incorporating collateral battlefield elements, like a civilian populace, challenges leaders to cognitively analyze the situation and think beyond the battle drill.

On the individual level, **leaders should develop personal cognitive battle drills that better prepare them for the mental challenges of combat.** They should rehearse exactly what words they will use to report an initial contact and what guidance they anticipate issuing in the opening moments of a battle. These drills create neural circuitry that is familiar to the brain when the actual event happens, thus making it easier to execute with calm and confidence.

These drills serve as a personal routine that primes the individual to control stress, sense subconscious patterns, engage cognitive problem solving, and lead with emotional control. Then, by adding the element of physical danger or stress to the scenario, leaders can adapt to perform the cognitive thinking despite emotional distraction.[53] David Rock notes, "People who succeed under pressure have learned to be in a place of high arousal but maintain a quiet mind, so that they can still think clearly. Over time and with practice, this capacity can become an automatic resource. The brain can be wired to deal better with emotions."[54] This adaptation will develop mental fitness for leaders that may prove to be crucial in the unit's future battles.

Leaders must learn where they should position themselves on the battlefield to facilitate their cognitive responsibilities. Despite mission, terrain, or movement technique, leaders must discern what position allows them to survey all aspects of the fight.[55] As much as possible, they should directly observe their Soldiers and get information real time without compromising their ability to keep a macro view. Conversely, Soldiers expect to see their leaders at the proverbial "front" and cannot respect leaders who are never among them. **Finding this balance is part of what makes leadership an art.**

Most importantly, all leaders have the responsibility to build a database of professional knowledge that will assist them in creating insight during stressful situations. They do this by studying doctrine, seeking instruction from mentors, being self-critical about performance, recording new ideas, participating in thought exercises, discussing related concepts with peers, and reading professional works. A solid knowledge of history (long-term memory) will provide the prefrontal cortex (and working memory) with a vast array of tactical options from which to generate new solutions for the current fight. Coupled with an ever-expanding collection of personal experiences, a thorough knowledge of the military profession will enable leaders to find creative answers on the complex battlefield.

Conclusion

"The test of fitness to command is the ability to
think clearly in the face of unexpected contingency or opportunity."[56]

Combat involves a wide range of events, dangers, and sensory inputs that can easily overwhelm the unprepared mind. The first job of every soldier, regardless of rank, is to maintain his composure and react reflexively to the threat as required. Leaders, however, must go beyond the conditioned response to combat that is trained on the live-fire range. They must "zoom out" to adopt a macro-level view of the battle, quickly analyze the events occurring, decide on an appropriate response, coordinate complex systems, and then apply the appropriate leadership skills to accomplish the mission. These brain functions are among the most sophisticated processes that we humans can perform.

Leaders who do not protect their own cognitive function during combat will find themselves short of the biological resources necessary to win, and can place themselves and others at risk. In this sense, **knowing how to think could be a combat leader's most valuable tool.**

Citations and Notes

1   Evian Gordon, Ph.D., quoted in David Rock, Your Brain at Work: Strategies for Overcoming Distraction, Regaining Focus, and Working Smarter All Day Long (New York: HarperCollins, 2009), 105.

2   Rock, 107.

3   According to Columbia University, Program for the Imaging and Cognitive Sciences, "Functional MRI is based on the increase in blood flow to the local vasculature that accompanies neural activity in the brain." It allows scientists to observe what regions of the brain are activated in response to presented stimuli or during episodes associated with disorders like seizure activity and PTSD. Columbia University, Program for the Imaging and Cognitive Sciences, <http://www.fmri.org/fmri.htm> (8 March 2010). Other research methods used to map neural pathways include chemical tracing of neurotransmitters and cerebral interruption using surgical lesions. Joseph LeDoux, The Emotional Brain: The Mysterious Underpinnings of Emotional Life (New York: Simon & Schuster, 1996), 155.

4   Rock, Your Brain at Work, 57.

5   It is important to note that the theory of a "limbic system" is a contested topic in the arena of neuroscience because the term implies that there is one consolidated system that governs the emotional activities of the brain. Such a system has never been unequivocally proven. Therefore, I follow conventional science by using the term "limbic system" as a collective label for the processes that occur among the brain regions that independently influence fear response, memory recall, bodily reactions, and others.

6   Jonah Lehrer, How We Decide (New York: Houghton Mifflin Harcourt, 2009), 100.

7   American Health Assistance Foundation, <http://www.ahaf.org/ alzheimers/ about/understanding/anatomy-of-the-brain.html, April 2010> (14 March 2010).

8   Rand Swenson, M.D., Ph.D., Review of Clinical and Functional Neuroscience, chap. 11, online resource, Dartmouth Medical School, <http://www.dartmouth. edu/~rswenson/NeuroSci/chapter_11.html, 2006> (15 March 2010).

9   *Ibid.*, chap. 9, <http://www.dartmouth.edu/~rswenson/NeuroSci/ chapter_9. html>.

10 In this case, the optic nerves transmit visual data to the visual thalamus, which sends the information along two pathways to the amygdala. The quicker of the two is a direct link from the thalamus to the amygdala, resulting in rapid but less-detailed information about the threat. LeDoux refers to this system as "The Low Road." This is the instant that your mind recognizes a curved, slender object on the trail at your feet and springs your body into evading action. The slower data pathway routes the information from the thalamus, first through the frontal cortex, and then to the amygdala. This is "The High Road," termed so because the frontal cortex analyzes the data in detail and makes a more precise appraisal of the threat. If the object at your feet is not a snake but a stick, then this is the moment you consciously realize your error, laugh at yourself, and continue hiking. But of course, "It is better to have treated a stick as a possible snake than not to have responded to a possible snake." LeDoux, The Emotional Brain, 163-66.

11 Swenson, Review of Clinical and Functional Neuroscience, chapter 11.

12 Brian Wandell, "Looking into the Brain," podcast lecture, Stanford University, 29 April 2008, downloaded 26 February 2009.

13 *Ibid.*

14 Lehrer, How We Decide, 152.

15 John Case, David Rock, "Neuroscience in the Workplace," 18 February 2007, podcast (7 April 2009).

16 David Rock, "Your Brain at Work—David Rock's new book," 8 October 2009, podcast (9 October 2009).

17 Joseph LeDoux, "Fearful Brains in an Anxious World," podcast, The New York Academy of Sciences: Science and the City Podcast, 21 November 2008 (7 February 2010).

18 Laurence Gonzales, Deep Survival: Who Lives, Who Dies, and Why (London: W.W. Norton, 2003), 229.

19 Lehrer paraphrase of Antonio Damasio description of the mind's reaction to danger. Jonah Lehrer, Proust Was a Neuroscientist (New York: First Mariner, 2008), 19. 20. Brigadier General S.L.A. Marshall, U.S. Army, Retired, Men Against Fire: The Problem of Battle Command in Future War (Alexandria: Byrrd, 1947), 48.

20 J.F.C. Fuller, as quoted in Marshall, Men Against Fire, 71.

21 Bruce K. Siddel, Sharpening the Warrior's Edge: The Psychology & Science

22 of Training (Belleville: PPCT Research Publications, 1995).

23 LeDoux, The Emotional Brain, 175.

24 Ibid.

25 Dave Grossman, Loren W. Christensen, On Combat: The Psychology and Physiology of Deadly Conflict in War and in Peace (USA: PPCT Research Publications, 2004), 88.

26 Ibid.

27 Ibid., 320.

28 *Ibid.*, 321.

29 Rock, Your Brain at Work, 112.

30 Rock,"Your Brain at Work," podcast.

31 Gonzales, Deep Survival, 44.

32 Paraphrase from General Patton's speech to the Third Army in England, 5 June

33 1944, published by Charles M. Province (Random House, 1988), 32. 33. Malcolm Gladwell (New York: Little, Brown, 2005), 208.

34 *Ibid.*

35 Rock, "Your Brain at Work," podcast.

36 Lehrer, 130.

37 *Ibid.*

38 *Ibid.*

39 *Ibid.*

40 Rock, Your Brain at Work, 40.

41 *Ibid.*, 81.

42 Lehrer, How We Decide, 23.

43 *Ibid.*, 38.

44 Rock, Your Brain at Work, 34.

45 *Ibid.*, 34.

46 *Ibid.*

47 *Ibid.*, 23.

48 *Ibid.*, 34.

49 Marshall, 116.

50 Committee on Opportunities in Neuroscience for Future Army Applications, National Research Council, Opportunities in Neuroscience for Future Army Applications (Washington, DC: National Academies Press, 2009), 20, <http://www.nap.edu/ catalog. php?record_id–12500> (19 May 2009).

51 It is important to note that exercise-induced stress is not the same as fear-induced stress. Fear-induced stress amplifies the effects of heart rate, blood pressure, and breathing and can severely impact the individual's ability to react with cognitive control. Accompanying combat skills with physical exertion, however, has proven to significantly improve the individual's ability to cope with fear-induced stress. Grossman, On Combat, 44.

52 The traditional term "stress shoot" refers to a shooting exercise where Soldiers participate in a physically stressful activity (e.g. pulling a weighted stretcher or sprinting) then immediately transition to a shooting exercise. The goal is to train the soldier to fire his weapon accurately despite the hindering effects of stress.

53 The use of Simunitions©, for example, has greatly improved military and law enforcement professionals' conditioning to combat. The effect of having to feel "real pain" in the training scenario creates a higher level of fear-induced stress than training exercises that do not incorporate physical pain. Grossman, On Combat, 36

54 Rock, Your Brain at Work, 115.

55 Major Thomas Siebold, U.S. Army, email to author, 3 May 2010.

56 Marshall, 117.

How Compassion Can Make or Break a Career

You might not have realized it, but there's an important date in the lives of your Soldiers that you should pay attention to. You don't know the exact time yet—it could be weeks, months, or years away—but it's out there. I'm talking about the day that each Soldier you lead raises his or her hand to reenlist for another term of service. It's a big day for them, and for the Army. And like it or not, everything you do influences whether or not they make that commitment.

Family & Army ... Competing Priorities

Several years ago, while in the hospital after the birth of our second child, I observed a Private First Class in uniform wandering the halls of the Labor & Delivery Floor. I casually inquired about his situation and discovered that his wife had their first child the day before, yet he had reported to work that morning and was fortunately able to break away to visit. That's right, *his first child was born on a Wednesday and someone made him come into work on Thursday.*

Leaders often make the mistake of measuring their unit's importance based on it's level of activity. The packed calendar, the stress of training events, and the surge of taskings make it easy to overlook the personal moments that matter most for the Soldiers involved. Leaders put the Army in conflict with their personal lives and leave it to them to sort out. Soldiers do indeed sort it out, but too often it's years down the road when it comes time to reenlist.

Who knows whether that new father had been told to come to work or if his supervisor was simply not aware of the circumstances. Regardless, situations like that can be immensely destructive to the family's loyalty to the Service and continued commitment to serve. If we can send Soldiers back from overseas deployment to be home for childbirth (which I've coordinated many times), then there is not a single reason to bring a Soldier back to work in the 5 … 7 … or even 14 days afterwards.

Compassion Matters

If the intent is to cancel that reenlistment date years in the future, disregarding significant personal milestones is a good way to do it. The same goes for times of personal crisis. It's tough to argue that the job can't be filled by someone else while a Soldier deals with the situation. The unit might sacrifice a few days of efficiency, but we might earn years of devoted service.

Here are a few other situations that leaders should strongly consider showing compassion when responding to:

- A complicated childbirth that will require numerous medical appointments.
- Illness or death of a family member, including extended family and grandparents.
- An unexpected financial hardship like a car crash or stolen identity.
- Times of spousal relationship difficulty or severe challenges with children.
- A Soldier's move to a new duty station, where having adequate time to get settled sets the tone for the family's time in the unit. (Come on, leaders, you do not need that Soldier at work the day after he signs-in to post. Figure out a way to manage without him for 10 days of Permissive TDY.)
- During scheduled leave, when Soldiers and families have been planning and looking forward to the time for themselves.
- After an unexpected career shift, like not being selected for promotion, receiving individual deployment orders, or being found medically unqualified for service.

Soldiers know that personal sacrifice is an inevitable part of military life … but everyone has a threshold. Leaders can go a long way towards keeping Soldiers and families away from that threshold by paying attention to the moments that matter, by being pragmatic about unit priorities, and by treating Soldiers with the same compassion the leaders themselves would hope to receive.

In a very literal sense, the future of the Service depends on it.

Section 3
Grow Your Team

How to Build a Team of "Yes Men"

Listening to one of Michael Hyatt's podcast episodes on creating team unity, my first reaction was, "We're good! The military has got this team alignment thing figured out. We're focused on the mission, we have a clear command structure, and we follow orders." But as Michael explained the steps to creating team alignment, he said that to get the most powerful results, leaders must:

Create an environment that is safe for dissent.

Ouch! Ok, that's not the first phrase most military members would use to describe their work environment. In fact, I think it's rare that I've seen a military leader who embraces dissent in the name of creating unity. I know I've never prioritized it.

The result? We get a team full of Yes Men who not only fail to speak up when they disagree with mundane issues, but are also trained to remain quiet in the face of critical decisions. If you want a team of folks like that, then make sure you do these things.

If you want to create a team full of Yes Men, then ...

Hire people who think just like you. If everyone in the room is nodding their heads in agreement, then no one is brainstorming the multitude of ways the plan can falter.

Interrupt your people. Nothing communicates disrespect like stopping someone mid-sentence to insert your wisdom. You're basically telling them that you're uninterested in their ideas and they should agree with you at every opportunity.

Tell your subordinates how to do their jobs. Perhaps your team members don't have adequate training or experience to achieve excellence. Maybe their method is not the way you would do it. It's ok, tell them exactly how to do their jobs and they'll get used to waiting for your guidance.

Give your opinion early and often. Michael Hyatt mentions how a leader can stifle an atmosphere of collaboration and inclusion by speaking his opinion early. When the leader poses an issue and immediately states his belief about the solution, everyone in the room will (consciously or subconsciously) bend their beliefs to align with his.

Deconstruct every suggestion people offer. Marshall Goldsmith in *What Got You Here Won't Get You There,* offers "20 Workplace Habits You Need to Break." One of which is "Starting your remarks with No, But, or However." He says,

> When you start a sentence with "no," "but," "however," or any variation thereof, no matter how friendly your tone or how many cute mollifying phrases you throw in to acknowledge the other person's feelings, the message to the other person is *You are wrong.*

Tell them they're wrong enough times and they'll say Yes to everything you say.

Assert your authority at every opportunity. If you still want a room full of Yes Men—and you don't think your team can see the rank on your chest which clearly exhibits your authority—then make sure you constantly tell them who's in charge.

Add too much value and get the last word. Similarly, put your two cents into every discussion and ensure that your subordinates leave the room with your guidance (certainly not their approved and encouraged idea) fresh in their minds. Marshall Goldsmith ranks "Adding too much value" as Bad Workplace Habit #2. He says that when leaders respond with, "*Good* *idea, but you should do it this way ...,*" then they destroy the subordinate's commitment to the idea while improving it only a little. What will that get you? "*Whatever you say, boss.*"

React with anger. Here's a surefire way to shut down communication and get people in line with "*Yes's.*" Responding to bad news with anger will make your team members think twice about bringing it to you. If you think your military mission can afford that hesitation, then anger is the way to go.

Don't recognize the credentials of others. Failing to acknowledge the education, experience, and proven success of your team members causes them to question whether their ideas are good enough to offer. It's easy for people to say, "*Well, the boss doesn't think any of us bring anything to the table, so why should we contribute?*"

Don't express gratitude. If you think "Selfless Service" also means "Thankless Service," then brush off every accomplishment as "just part of my people's duty to the mission." A thanks doesn't cost anything, but failure to offer thanks could cost your followers' drive to contribute to the team.

Don't ask for input or performance feedback. If you are completely satisfied with where you are as a team, and personally as a leader, then there's no need to get your team's opinion of your performance. Marshall Goldsmith may not be talking about you when he says, "Successful people are incredibly delusional about their achievements. Over 95 percent of the members in most successful groups believe that they perform in the top half of their group."

Bottom Line

Having a team full of Yes Men is perfectly ok ... as long as your skill as a leader is perfect enough to account for all the breakthrough ideas, seized opportunities, avoided catastrophes, and psychological cohesion that come from building an aligned and committed team. If you want that team instead, then do the opposite of everything above.

On Good Ideas and Hard Work

Have you ever looked at your team or organization and thought, "Wow, the people are working hard and we're doing so many good things ... but why doesn't it feel like we're a well-oiled machine by now?" I certainly have. And you've probably also been the one in the middle of the organization looking around you saying, "Despite all this good effort, why does it feel like we're spinning our wheels?"

Organizations that suffer from this problem often exhibit a common behavioral mistake: They take on too many good ideas and don't properly implement the ideas they do commit to. Reading Peter F. Drucker, the grandfather of modern business leadership and author of more than 35 books, I found some insight worth sharing.

Good Ideas Can Hurt

Military leaders have a hard time saying no to a good idea, even at the expense of stated priorities. Because we care so much about development, we evaluate the idea in light of its contributor instead of in light of the idea's usefulness to the unit. It's as if simply *having* a good idea is the benchmark of high performance. It's clearly not ... but we can't say no. Ideas get implemented, and people get run into the ground because of it.

In his bestseller from 1967, *The Effective Executive*, Peter Drucker focuses his analysis on the *effectiveness* of leaders and their organizations. He explains that effort is useless, perhaps destructive, if it does not support organizational priorities. This can happen easily in a culture that doesn't filter good ideas.

Drucker also draws a sharp line between talent and effectiveness:

… there seems to be little correlation between a man's effectiveness and his intelligence, his imagination or his knowledge. Brilliant men are often strikingly ineffectual; they fail to realize that the brilliant insight is not by itself achievement. They never have learned that insights become effectiveness only through hard systematic work.

So, the good ideas that proliferate from motivated individuals on the team are not enough to ensure success. The road from "Aha!" to AAR requires hard work, individually and systematically.

> Effectiveness is a habit; that is, a complex of practices. And practices can always be learned. Practices are simple, deceptively so; even a seven-year-old has no difficulty in understanding a practice. But practices are always exceedingly hard to do well. They have to be acquired, as we all learn the multiplication table; that is, repeated ad nauseam until "6 x 6 = 36" has become an unthinking, conditioned reflex, and firmly ingrained habit. Practices one learns by practicing and practicing and practicing again.

This advice applies on the rifle range as much as it does in the boardroom.

Accuracy Over Speed

But even after leaders create momentum to capitalize on good ideas, they must verify that the activity actually achieves the desired endstate. This is organizational effectiveness.

Consider marksmanship as an analogy. A new squad leader joins the ranks of a platoon, bringing with him a wealth of experience for the unit's upcoming deployment. He is also a shooting hobbyist with years of practice at speed shooting. He is motivated to contribute, and upon arriving sets about teaching his new squad how to quicken their response time with the rifle. The Platoon Leader and Platoon Sergeant value the energy he's bringing to the unit and don't hold him back.

The squad spends hours upon hours focused on making faster rifle shots. The Soldiers are quicker for sure, but their accuracy has only improved a little. And now it's time to deploy.

Two problems: First, the good idea wasn't properly implemented. What good is speed if the shots miss? A deliberate assessment of the program would have noted that. Second, the unit's mission in the approaching deployment will be mounted escort, not dismounted patrolling. An effective training plan would have focused on convoy operations and marksmanship with mounted weapon systems.

Implementing a Good Idea

Leaders bear the responsibility of distilling the best ideas from the organization and crafting them into effective activity. In brainstorming the topic, I settled on four questions leaders should ask in the pursuit of effectiveness:

1. Based on our endstate (effects we want to achieve), what practices should we focus on?
2. What is the best, most efficient program to teach those practices?
3. What methods can we use to measure the outcome of the training?
4. How can we measure the resulting effect to achieve our mission?

These questions strip away the excitement of a good idea and evaluate it against the unit's priorities, the key step to reducing ineffective activity.

Scaling Effectiveness

Drucker also mentions effectiveness as a "complex of practices." Practices in the military range from reflexive and instinctive at the squad level to complex and interconnected at higher levels. In training for organizational effectiveness, leaders must determine what activity (warfighting as well as staff practices) they can make reflexive and what must remain—for lack of a better term—fluid. Executing battle drills in an operations center should be reflexive; generating ideas during planning, fluid. Reporting logistics status to higher headquarters, reflexive; tailoring the resupply packages to maximize efficiency, fluid.

A leader's thorough understanding of the organization will allow him to connect ideas to habits that support the mission. All else is wasted effort.

Having Influence that Echoes

One interesting aspect of hosting The Military Leader is that I get to see the website's viewership stats. Unlike counterinsurgency efforts, the effects of online writing can be clearly measured. Google Analytics provides detailed reports on the number and locations of visitors, time spent on pages, number of shares, and a lot more data that I don't get into.

What's neat is when people discover and share some of the older posts, causing a spike in that page's traffic for a day or two. This happened recently, and I found it fascinating that thoughts I had months or even years ago were continuing to provide meaning and value for people. A metaphor for leadership emerged.

Rippling Influence

Leadership is unmistakably about influence. Passionate leaders spend night and day discovering ways to improve their organizations and have an impact that endures. The best leaders inspire growth that survives their tenure, even their lifetime, and continues to echo positive influence through time.

Some leaders achieve this with charisma and élan. Others' influence persists due to their stalwart performance despite extreme hardship. And still others exude a quiet confidence and exhibition of talent that transmits lessons throughout each day.

But what every successful leader has achieved is an ability to relate to the led–to display some quality worth admiring and remembering which causes their influence to propagate beyond a single engagement. In the best case, followers jot down a note or strain to memorize the leader's words and their lives are consequently changed because of it.

Leading for Longevity

So, how can military leaders break through the modern-day "noise" to achieve lasting influence that matters? Here are a few thoughts:

Connect at their level. Soldiers comment all the time about leaders who get stuck on lofty messages with no relevance to "life on the ground." Take a few moments to envision life from your audience's perspective and consider their daily challenges. Shape your advice based on their reality, not yours.

Clarify and rehearse. Military leaders, particularly commanders, do a lot of talking off the cuff. There's constant opportunity to ad lib, which sometimes leads to a muddled message. Prevent this by taking the time to formalize your leadership thoughts and craft them into talking points that you can refer to during teachable moments.

Twitterize your message. Be concise. When you craft those talking points, make them brief, succinct, and pithy. Write them in a conversational tone that's repeatable, not an academic tone with too many ideas in one sentence.

Make it timeless. If you want your message to echo beyond the engagement, phrase it in a way that's more general in nature and applicable to other situations. For example, change *"It's extremely important that we thoroughly check these vehicles to prevent accidents and maintain a high readiness rating"* to *"Do your duty with precision and care, and you will save lives."*

Maximize group engagement. Group settings and formations can get dull really quick if the message isn't captivating and brief. Approach these opportunities with deliberate care and avoid going in without a plan. Use guest speakers, competitions, examples, and jokes to communicate message that last.

Stick to your strengths. I once had a commander who didn't like to curse in conversation, but would try to connect with Soldiers using curse words. It was a dismal failure. His timing, inflection, and word choice were all flawed and he sounded fake and insincere. People will remember what feels emotionally genuine, so make sure your message aligns with who you are.

Five Steps to Effectively Communicating Your Message

Information is clearly an important part of combat operations, but what about back at home station? How can leaders communicate their message to the organization to do things like meet unit goals, achieve a shared vision, or simply influence subordinate behavior?

Whether dealing with an unplanned crisis or trying to achieve incremental change, leaders must actively communicate their message to the organization, or else its members will draw their own (possibly uninformed) conclusions and fall victim to rumors and misinformation. **Leaders who remain silent end up surrendering their influence to people and entities that do not have the team's best interests at heart.**

Here are 5 steps that leaders can take to communicate their message and gain the information initiative:

Step 1: Identify Your Audience — *empathetic communication*

This step seems obvious, but leaders must identify exactly whom they want to influence, acknowledging that each audience may require a different message. Are you talking to Soldiers? Families? Adjacent units? Only the high-performing leaders? Only the "at-risk" individuals? Soldiers transitioning to civilian life?

Audiences will react differently to the same message because they hear it from varying perspectives. It's a mistake to think, "I'm the leader, so it's everyone else's responsibility to understand my message, not the other way around."

Step 2: Develop Your Message

This step is more than simply refining what you want to say. Your message is an intentional statement of your leadership—a translation of how you will apply your character, talents, and personality to the given situation. Though we all use prior experience to inform and shape our actions, leaders cannot assume that what has worked before will work again.

Write down the key points you want to communicate and scrutinize them in light of the current environment. Will subordinates understand your perspective? Is the message outdated or boring? Will it capture their attention and inspire change? Get feedback from trusted advisors to make sure you're on the right track.

Step 3: Make it Digestible and Actionable

Chances are you've written your message in a way that's easiest for YOU to understand, which may not be the easiest for everyone else to understand. ("Big thinkers" often succumb to this tendency when translating their grandiose visions.) Audiences don't live inside your head and won't have perspective on the process you endured to arrive at the message you're bringing.

Make your message simple, clear, and digestible. Include a story, metaphor, or example to relate your message to real life. If you are casting a vision for the organization, be sure to include details that will resonate with the different groups who will be a part of it.

Next, make the message actionable, especially if you are giving guidance or shaping the road ahead. Make a list, identify milestones, and describe changes that will occur, all of which will translate your perspective into tangible outcomes.

Step 4: Identify the Conduits and Catalysts

Every organization has people who connect across multiple groups and engage with large numbers of people. They are often extroverts who also represent the archetype of the population. You'll want to craft your message with these people in mind because they can multiply its effectiveness, particularly by influencing the fence-sitters. Consider engaging them and gaining their support before you publicize your message.

Step 5: Plan and Execute an Engagement Strategy

Now that you've developed a clear message targeted at the right audience, decide when and how often to deliver your message. Will it be part of a speech? Is it a conversational message? Is it formal guidance, requiring a meeting or memo?

If it is a core message or an organizational priority, plan to sound like a broken record. Here's a good rule of thumb: **If it doesn't feel like you've repeated your message at least a thousand times, you probably haven't gotten it across.** You may get tired of saying it, but there are always new people to influence, particularly in the high turnover of military units.

Consider these methods to communicate your message:

- At formations and gatherings
- As the opening discussion at meetings
- Through your leaders
- When visiting subordinate headquarters and training events
- In emails to the organization's leaders/members
- During physical training with team members
- At morale events (particularly for family-related messages)
- On the organization's social media sites (Facebook, Twitter, website)

One useful engagement strategy is the 3x5 Method. Pick the three most important/influential groups in your organization and commit to transmitting your message to them at least five separate times.

Finally, remember to routinely connect people back to The Why. Simon Sinek brings this point home in his TED talk "How Great Leaders Inspire Action," where he emphasizes that what inspires people to action is being reminded of why they started in the first place. Remind people of why they joined the service, recount inspirational historical examples, and highlight courage.

10 Ways to Start a Conversation About Leadership

Vince Lombardi wisely quipped, *"The man on top of the mountain didn't fall there."* Success does not happen by accident … and neither does becoming a leader. The road to meaningful influence is marked by deliberate steps to acquire knowledge, gain experience, and engage in ways that specifically relate to leadership. Followers can do this on their own, but leaders have a tacit responsibility to grow other leaders and must find ways to further the leadership development of those around them.

Bringing Leadership to Life

Even in military circles, most conversations do not naturally drift towards topics of leadership. People can remember the last conversation they had about sports, but probably not the last conversation they had about leading by example, or delegating or ethical decision-making.

If the team members are to grow in these areas, someone (the leader) will have to take an active role in generating original thought and guiding them towards insight. Here are some practical ways to get that conversation going:

Use face-to-face time throughout your day to engage those around you. Ask any one of these questions to groups or individuals you encounter:

- "Who inspires you and why?"

- "What is one leadership-related skill that you are working to improve?"
- "If you could meet one military leader from history, who would it be and why?"
- "Name one leadership challenge you faced this week and how did you handle it?"
- "What is the worst leadership experience you've ever had and what did you learn from it?"
- "What was the leadership environment like in your last unit and how does it compare to this one?"
- "What do you look for in a good leader? How about in a good follower?"
- "What is your all time favorite leadership quote?"
- "Describe a mentor who has had a significant impact on you as a leader."
- Briefly explain a challenging situation you face in your own position, then ask how they would handle it.

Post a weekly or daily quote on a dry erase board in your unit area or outside your office and ask people to comment on it. Start with this one: *"If your actions inspire others to dream more, learn more, do more and become more, you are a leader."* – John Quincy Adams

Take advantage of "team time." Maximize the time that your team is assembled and listening, like close-out formations. Give them something formative to walk away with, not just a list of warnings about staying out of trouble.

Books are a great primer for conversation. When people stop by your desk for routine matters, peak their curiosity by leaving a leadership book or article out and visible. Be ready to give them the quick takeaways.

In a less subtle way, ask questions related to the books you're reading. "Hey, have you read *The 21 Irrefutable Laws of Leadership*? Maxwell talks about 'The Law of the Lid' and how team effectiveness is determined by leadership ability. What do you think?"

Make good content readily available to the team. Make a binder of leadership articles you read and place it in a common area for your team to browse while on CQ duty or waiting for meetings. Then ask people to read, highlight, and make their own notes in the margins.

Similarly, consider assigning a leadership-related concept or word for the week and encourage subordinate team members to use it in their conversations. Examples might be *vision, value-based leadership, leading with strengths, training to standard*, or any of the Army values.

Maximize social media. Most people could make better use of their social media connections as leader development tools. Start a leadership conversation in your Facebook feed and see where it goes.

Weave leadership into daily activity. There's almost never a bad time to talk about leadership. Meetings, PT sessions, walking to chow. You don't need to drag it out, just take a moment to direct the conversation towards something meaningful instead of the typical banter. You can also include leadership references in your emails. Maybe there's a particular quote or experience you can cite to reinforce a lesson.

Let someone else do the talking. Find a few TED talks about leadership and use them to prime discussions that relate to your unit or the challenges you face. This might be a good method for those who are less comfortable with leading a discussion group or starting a leadership conversation out of nowhere.

Making leader development part of your day is not as challenging (or weird) as you might think. People feel enlightened, motivated, even inspired when others add value that personally grows them. Reach out. Start a conversation. Ask a question. You'll not only reveal lessons that your followers might have overlooked, but most importantly, you will develop a habit of looking at the world through a lens of leadership. And that is a priceless skill.

Stop Creating Confusion and Start Providing Answers

There's nothing more frustrating for a subordinate headquarters than to receive an order that lacks context on the situation or fails to provide the resources needed for execution. It seems that some people advance in their careers and forget what it's like to serve at the lower levels. One example provides a good lesson on how higher leaders and staff can enable their organizations instead of causing confusion.

Consider this Example

I got a mass email from the division headquarters in preparation for an upcoming visit from a four-star commanding general. The email gave instructions to the units and individuals that the general would visit, giving us the pertinent times and locations of the visit. Then it said, "Ensure that all personnel have read and understand the general's training guidance for this fiscal year, as well as his published policy on sexual harassment prevention."

My natural reaction was, *"Ok, where can I find those documents?"* But the higher staff did not attach them to the email or make it easy for me to complete their task. Instead of providing answers, they created confusion. Thus, I spent the next 20 minutes searching for the appropriate documents so I could review them myself (and then send them on to my subordinates).

Lesson

Effective staff organizations provide answers, not more questions. Take the perspective of the people you're leading and shape your products to make it easy to follow your orders ... *even if it means more work for you!* Serve and enable the people you lead and you will accomplish the overall mission more efficiently and effectively.

Why "It Is What It Is" is a Stupid Phrase

It's Baghdad, 2007. I'm a company commander deploying to a contentious area during the height of The Surge. As my unit starts to shadow the unit we're replacing, and I spend time with my counterpart and his battalion's staff, I begin to hear a new phrase pop up: "*It is what it is.*"

I wouldn't have thought much of it, but I heard that response from numerous members of the unit and applied to all types of discussion topics. My buddies and boss picked up on it, too. I heard "*It is what it is*" so much that I began to think it was an approved mentality of the unit, a sanctioned mindset.

Well, my observation was incontrovertibly validated the moment I heard the unit's battalion commander speak. He led a handover brief for us that covered the major events and efforts of his unit's tour, and I heard "*It is what it is*" more times than I can count. "*The Iraqi Army unit you're partnering with can't show up to an operation on time, but it is what it is.*" "*We've got a really small post here, so parking will be tight. It is what it is.*" "*We took a lot of casualties in this area, so you should be prepared for that. It is what it is.*"

He used the phrase to explain (or rather, excuse) action and inaction, misfortune and blessing, success and failure. And as I alluded, the phrase had evolved from words to a mindset and permeated the command climate in the unit. Ever since that interaction in 2007, I've been passively tuned-in for the phrase and have heard it several times each year in follow-on assignments.

Why It's Stupid

The problem with *"It is what it is"* is that it abdicates responsibility, shuts down creative problem solving, and concedes defeat. A leader who says *"It is what it is"* is a leader who faced a challenge, couldn't overcome it, and explained away the episode as an inevitable, unavoidable force of nature ("We are at the mercy of the gods"). Replace *"It is what it is"* with *"This resulted because I failed to do _____"* and you get an entirely different discussion.

The phrase is stupid enough when rationalizing insufficient performance, but it's especially damaging when *"It is what it is"* is used in framing a response to a problem. *"Well, that route to the objective is blocked. Guess we can't use it. It is what it is." We need indirect fire support, but the terrain here is too uneven to place the guns. It is what it is." "Those new IEDs are cutting through our vehicles pretty badly, but we're still waiting for the up-armored packages to arrive. It is what it is."*

"It is what it is" is an admission that the problem is too hard and suppresses the attitude that leads to creative, unseen solutions. Even if a leader has racked his brain and combed his own experience for a solution to the challenge, yet can't find one, he should realize that his unit's people contain a wealth of unique experiences and perspectives to contribute. *"It is what it is"* negates their value. It says *"We can't,"* which is the antithesis of everything we espouse to make our military capable and lethal.

An EntreLeadership podcast interview with Sebastian Bailey brings home the point. He said if you show people the shape of a square and ask them what it is, they invariably answer *"square."* But, if you instead ask them *what it could be*, then a world of possibilities emerge: The frame of a house. A baseball diamond. A graduation cap. The new question (which originated from a mindset of possibility rather than defeat) reframes the mind to look for solutions without boundaries, exactly the type of thinking we want our leaders to demonstrate.

Caveat ...

While you'll never hear me use the phrase *"It is what it is,"* there is value in maintaining a portion of your attitude that is stoic in nature. Know what you can control and what you can't control. And the first thing to accept that you can't control is the past. Shooting schools teach a principle: *"Once the bullet leaves the barrel, it's gone. You can do nothing more to affect where it goes. So, let it go and focus on perfecting the next shot."*

It's the same with life and leadership. Don't dwell on what's happened. Take responsibility, learn the appropriate lessons, and get moving to the next objective. Doing otherwise is a distraction.

Similarly, don't waste your time trying to change something that won't help you achieve your mission or stated priorities. Allocate your effort appropriately, not in crusades that leave your people worse off. For example, *"It is what it is"* says there's no way that you can get the Secretary of Defense to speak at your battalion ball, but you spend personal and organizational time and energy trying to make it happen. Meanwhile, your unit fails to prepare for the upcoming training center rotation and falls flat on its face. Not cool. Better to have spent that creative energy on finding unique ways to make your unit lethal.

Bottom Line

Followers take cues from their leaders. Leaders who adopt the *"It is what it is"* attitude demonstrate two qualities to their people: They won't accept responsibility for what has happened, and they won't get creative in shaping what will happen. That's not the kind of leader that makes our military successful.

Five Questions That Can Save You from Disaster

I admit it. The fault was entirely my own. I had let myself get comfortable and now I was short on time, resources, energy, and just about everything needed to make a successful operation. And I could have prevented it.

At the time, I was a company commander in Baghdad and the last few days had shown a sharp increase in enemy attacks. The entire brigade area of operations was increasing in intensity and commanders were making decisions about how to react.

My battalion commander informed me that there was some discussion about shifting a portion of my company to another combat outpost, but that nothing had been decided. He said that during the morning's update, the brigade commander had asked about the feasibility of moving my assets, but then tabled it for another discussion. *"I don't think he wants to move you. Don't worry about it for now,"* my commander relayed quickly as he rolled out to assess the fight.

So, I didn't ... and that was my mistake. I had been up for nearly 24 hours and my fatigued inner monologue told me that the current situation wouldn't change, so there was nothing for me to do.

Change of Plans

As one might expect in a post about hard-learned lessons, the situation changed. My commander sent me an email in the middle of the next morning's update: *"Change of plans. Brigade commander wants you to move north. He's talking 12 hours from now. Better get to work."*

I had lost 8 hours of useable planning and prep time because I failed to anticipate that I'd be told to move. The battlefield conditions had pointed to this course of action as a smart decision, and I'd even received an informal warning about the possibility ... but I didn't act. Consequently, I scrambled to inform the platoon leaders, coordinate with battalion, and put together a hasty plan. Worse, the company's Soldiers had to break their backs to make the directed movement timeline.

Preventing Disaster

How have you been caught off guard by something you could have anticipated? What indicators were present that should have informed you changes were coming?

For me, the fact that my brigade commander even mentioned the move should have been enough to set things in motion. He had a habit of floating ideas to commanders and staff, letting them marinate, then making a decision later on. At that point, I could have gotten the jump on things by warning my own people about the possibility, then identifying what would have to happen if we did get the call.

> *"There's absolutely no reason for us to assume ... that the Germans are mounting a major offensive. The weather is awful and their supplies are low. The Germans haven't mounted a winter attack since Frederick the Great. Therefore I believe that's exactly what they're going to do. I want you [the staff] to start making contingency plans for pulling out of our eastward attack, changing directions 90 degrees, and moving up to Luxembourg. ... Don't look so stunned, gentlemen."* (from *Patton*, 1970)

I realize now that it doesn't take much to anticipate events like I experienced. A few moments of reflection can cue you in to the key indicators a crisis hits. And asking hard questions will force you and your team to acknowledge the situation you face.

• 5 Questions •

Here are five questions that I ask when I'm in the middle of something important, or when I feel like I'm getting too comfortable with the situation:

1. What am I assuming that might not be true or may change later?
2. What other courses of action could emerge?
3. How much time would I have to react to a new course of action?
4. What assets would I need in place to adequately respond?
5. Who else needs to ask and answer these questions?

I've found that these questions force me to open my mind about what else is out there that could affect me and those I'm leading. They make me step outside my own perspective and evaluate the situation from the decision makers' point of view, as well as those in my sphere of influence who affect change. This short process serves as a brainstorming session to identify vulnerabilities, make the unknown known, and prepare for or prevent disaster.

And finally, it's key that the leader be the one to engage in this process. No one else has a better understanding of the scope of issues facing a unit or team, nor can anyone else create the mental space from the minutia needed to sense all that is happening.

Systems That Strangle

Last year, my wife and I invested many hours in the process of researching and purchasing a used car. The fun phase of test driving and haggling over, we moved into the not-so-fun phase of paperwork. The sales agent, who had come in on his day off to sell us this car, was eager to get us out the door and hurried to assemble papers for our signature.

"Here is your purchase order. Here is the total. This is the warranty brochure." All the standard forms. Then he highlighted, "And here is a disclosure so we can call you in the future." Wait a minute, we thought as we read through the form in detail, "It says that your dealership can contact us about special offers, too. We'd prefer not to get those."

"Oh, no," he said. "This just lets me do a follow-up call in six months to make sure you're happy with the purchase. We won't bombard you with any offers."

My response stymied him for a moment, "Yeah, that's ok. Believe me, I'll call you if there's anything wrong. I'd rather not sign it." Not only had he not needed a signed disclosure to call me during the buying process we'd just navigated for the last week, but this car wasn't even his dealership's make. It was a trade-in that didn't matter to his company. There was no need to follow up.

"Well, it's really no big deal. Everyone signs this form. It's part of the packet."

"Is it required to buy the car?" I asked. He responded in the negative.

"Good," I affirmed, "Then I'm more comfortable not signing it."

Interestingly, 20 minutes later we sat down with a very nice lady from the finance department who presented the same form for our signature. It was evident that not signing this disclosure statement was throwing them a curve ball. *What do you mean they don't want to sign the form??? They have to! It's part of the process.*

In the end, we stuck to our guns and avoided a year's worth of phone calls about special offers. But I also walked away with a lesson about processes, systems, and inflexibility.

"Check[list], please"

Now, the dealership folks were quite nice, very capable, and highly efficient with the process they had established. I didn't see it personally, but there was probably a checklist somewhere to guide the sales people. As long as all the pieces fell into place, they could tick off one sale after another according to a proven procedure.

Test drive … done. Price haggle … done. Warranty pitch … done. Purchase Order … done.

And maybe they had a few branch plans to account for routine deviations like insufficient credit or the addition of a roof rack. But, step off of the prescribed path to buying their car and they have to check with the manager.

Think about the processes that guide your life, both the formal ones designed to shape your work and the informal ones you've created to guide your personal time. If you're in the military, you don't have to look far to find a checklist … and it might be one that has lethal consequences if not followed. (In the aviation world, knowing flight checklists is an absolute necessity. But pilots must also know just how far they can deviate from those parameters in unplanned situations.)

Exploring for a moment, here's why we like the processes and checklists that fill our lives:

- They give us confidence that the system we are using is the most efficient.
- They imply that people before us have already ironed-out all the mistakes.
- They make it easier to train new or inexperienced team members.
- They allow us to operate within a safe construct, letting us avoid change and unnecessary risk.
- They give credibility to our activity, even if that activity is misaligned or not relevant. (*"I know we're not getting the results we want, but we're following the SOP."*)
- They give us a known perspective through which to view complex problems, which prevents us from seeing alternate approaches or generating new insights.

While processes allow us to efficiently execute tasks within a predictable system, they can also stifle. There exists an intangible line where the procedures we rely on begin to dilute both individual cognitive agility and collective organizational adaptability. Teams and their members take fewer risks and close themselves to new insights when they have processes to protect them. It's not intentional, it's a function of our innate propensity to seek homeostasis — a comfortable, predictable environment.

General Stanley McChrystal tackles this dilemma in his book, *Team of Teams*:

> The pursuit of "efficiency" — getting the most with the least investment of energy, time, or money—was once a laudable goal, but being effective in today's world is less a question of optimizing for a known (and relatively stable) set of variables than responsiveness to a constantly shifting environment. Adaptability, not efficiency, must become our central competency.

The takeaway here is twofold.

First, **take a moment to evaluate your own organization for processes that make your people comfortable.** Does your team espouse checklists over creativity? Could they adapt to a new, unplanned environment? When was the last time they were tested in a complex, ambiguous situation? If you think they have drifted into an area of complacency, shake things up. Present your people with dynamic scenarios that will reveal both their knowledge of the processes and their willingness to think beyond the checklist.

Second, **evaluate your own behavior as you pursue your goals.** Are you the type of person who challenges the systems you interact with? Would you have signed the dealership's disclosure form because *"they set the rules and have expert knowledge about what is required?"*

General Colin Powell has apt advice:

> Don't be buffaloed by experts and elites. Experts often possess more data than judgment. Elites can become so inbred that they produce hemophiliacs who bleed to death as soon as they are nicked by the real world.

History's most well-respected visionaries showed a committed resistance to the status quo, an unwillingness to blindly accept the hierarchies of life, an inspirational vision for shaping their environment, and a penchant for observing the masses and doing the opposite.

Is that you?

Six Ways to Enhance Your Close-Out Formation

The muscular but exhausted Soldiers maneuvered back and forth, looking for some advantage that would lead to victory. They had applied every hand-to-hand fighting skill they had to become the final two Soldiers in the pit after starting with 25 competitors. The rookie Private from Bravo Company then surprised the seasoned Staff Sergeant from Headquarters and launched him over the edge of the pit, causing an uproar from Bravo and securing bragging rights for the next month.

Doesn't sound like your typical close-out formation, does it?

The battalion commander had ordered each company to offer up 5 Soldiers at the monthly close-out formation challenge, but the teams didn't know what the competition was until after they were selected. It was a brilliant way to reinforce a crucial aspect of the unit's Vision Statement, *"Be ready to fight, anytime, anywhere."*

Most units view close-out formations simply as a venue to communicate information and give the mandatory safety brief. But with a little creativity, leaders can turn them into competitive, team-building events that build cohesion and give permanency to the leader's message.

Here are a few ideas.

Medal of Honor Citations

Nothing brings the team together like connecting today's service to yesterday's sacrifices. One great way to do this is to recount a Medal of Honor citation to the assembled troops. Sometimes no follow-up comment is necessary, as the impact of these stories of valor is often self-evident. But, you may want to connect the citation to some specific aspect of the unit or your command philosophy. To change it up, you can also select a different Soldier to read the citation each time.

I used the book *Medal of Honor: Portraits of Valor Beyond the Call of Duty*, which consistently resonated with the Soldiers.

Individual and Unit Challenges

As I related at the beginning, combatives are a surefire way to get the team riled up. There is no limit to how creative you can get with competitive events, physical or otherwise. Here are several ideas from my battalion, where we did individual and team competitions every month and the commander awarded a unit trophy:

- Obstacle course races in combat gear
- Pugil stick, boxing, and combatives challenges
- Good old-fashioned tug-o-war
- Round robin of CrossFit exercises for time or max repetitions
- Weapons assembly and functions check (and other critical skill-related tasks)
- Military vehicle push

Learn from Your Own

The years of war since 2001 have created a wealth of combat knowledge in our ranks. Reach out to your seasoned NCOs and Valor Award recipients and ask them to share a combat experience or hard-won lesson during close-out formation. It will not only earn them individual respect, but also foster a collective respect of the unit's capability.

Learn from Others

Guest speakers are another way to break out of the norm. You can invite the military leaders in your chain of command to speak from a perspective that the Soldiers wouldn't normally hear. (For example, bring down the Division Command Sergeant Major to talk about leadership, not motorcycle safety or drug use). But, if you want to drive home a lesson about safe behavior, ask the local Mothers Against Drunk Driving chapter to speak, or perhaps an escorted inmate who would have made different decisions. One time the close-out formation featured a policeman and a lawyer to give a firsthand account of how painful (and expensive) a DUI can be.

Recognize Your Own

It's nothing new to present awards at close-out formations, but you may want to highlight successes that would normally go unnoticed. Subordinate leaders can offer input on how their Soldiers are making a difference. Highlight hard work on a big project, volunteer work in the community, or how well a Soldier did on the fitness test. This method has the effect of bringing public recognition down to the Soldier level and gives credit to the folks are doing the hard work day-to-day.

If Nothing Else …

A buddy helped remind me of a priceless lesson he picked up years ago:

> Never miss an opportunity to talk to your assembled troops. When they're in formation and the First Sergeant asks if you have anything to say, always take the chance to teach an object lesson, encourage them, reinforce your command philosophy, or simply thank them for their hard work.

10 Easy Ways to Develop Your Leaders

You're overthinking it! Leader development doesn't have to be the big "thing" it sounds like when you say it.

When I became a platoon leader, I struggled with what type of development program to implement. Should I create a formal development plan with events and steps? Or should I simply model effective leadership and hope the Soldiers learn by example? I engaged a mentor on the topic, who gave me priceless advice that I remember to this day.

She said, "Just look for *teachable moments.*"

Too often, leaders adopt the belief that leader development has to be a lengthy program that takes hours or weeks to develop. The "unit leader development program" sounds like a monstrous effort that integrates technical training, tactical education, lofty discussions, resource products, and lots of time. Most of us shudder when we think about having to create one.

Here's the unfortunate result: Our flawed perception of leader development consequently prevents us from doing ANYTHING.

Consider these facts about leader development:

- It's more important than anything else you'll do
- You've already got the tools to develop your leaders
- THEY aren't too busy to get involved
- YOU aren't too busy to get involved

- They WANT you to teach them
- It can take as little as a few minutes, with almost no prep time

While you may have an overall plan for the path you'll take your leaders on, you should simplify how you approach the engagements. Here are 10 easy ways you can develop your leaders:

1. **Teach the basics again.** There's always value in reminding us how much we've forgotten.
2. **Tell war stories.** Your subordinates want to hear about your experiences and will apply your lessons to their own perspective.
3. **Discuss a quote.** Everyone has favorite quotes. Pick one and spend ten minutes discussing it. Ask the team to share relevant examples from their own experiences.
4. **Assign homework.** Give your team a topic to review and present.
5. **Highlight history.** Find valuable, perhaps inspirational events in history to share. (Medal of Honor citations are very effective in connecting the team with purpose and legacy.)
6. **Form resource scouts.** Divvy up multiple websites for your team to watch daily for good content to share.
7. **Invite guest speakers.** Ask subject matter experts or even higher leaders to speak to your team.
8. **Watch a video.** Find inspiring videos (TED, for example) or watch public speeches of your organization's leaders (CEOs, Generals, etc.).
9. **Review an article.** Professional journals provide excellent resources for discussion. Examples: Military Review, Joint Forces Quarterly, Infantry Magazine, etc. The Military Writers Guild is a fantastic place to cull useful content.
10. **Create a scenario-driven event.** Assign your team a tactical problem to solve and present to the group. It's as simple as grabbing a map and asking, "How would you seize this hill with an infantry platoon?"

The events don't have to be stand-alone. Consider opening a meeting with a short professional discussion. Or if it's a busy period, do a brown-bag lunch centered on a discussion topic. You can also integrate teaching moments into physical training or formation time.

Have We Removed Leadership from Leader Development?

Every year, new command teams spend thoughtful hours crafting the words that will precisely convey their version of unit success. This intent typically reaches the service members in the form of an organizational mission statement or "Unit Vision." And if your experience is anything like mine, leader development takes center stage. When those command teams brief their vision to the unit, the slides inevitably include phrases like these:

"Developing leaders is our #1 priority."
"Leader Development is in everything we do."
"The heart of this unit is its leaders."
"Good leadership is our most important asset."

Sound about right?

But when was the last time you participated in a unit leader development event that was focused on the practice of leadership? Not doctrine, not staff processes, not command supply discipline ... leadership! It's probably been a while.

It's been a while because collectively we have compartmentalized the study of leadership to the schoolhouse. We've also adopted the belief that training events fulfill the requirement to develop leaders. When *Leader Development is in everything we do,"* going to the range is leader development; so is doing physical training (PT) and inspecting vehicles.

Leader development has evolved to encompass everything except the very activity its name implies—teaching our people *how* to be good leaders.

Allow me to explain why this has occurred and what you can do about it.

A Succession of Skills

Developing leaders is the bedrock of sustaining a capable, multigenerational military. Technologies come and go, but it's our people who make the decisive difference. And the mandate to develop those people is quite clear. Take a look at the Army's guidance on developing leaders:

> Accomplishing the current mission is not enough—the leader is responsible for developing individuals and improving the organization for the near- and long-term. (1, ADP 6-22, *Army Leadership*)

> Unit training and leader development are the Army's life-blood. Army leaders train units to be versatile. They develop subordinate leaders—military and Army civilians—to be competent, confident, agile, and adaptive using the Army leader development model. Units and leaders master individual and collective tasks required to execute the unit's designed capabilities and accomplish its mission. (1, ADP 7-0, *Training Units and Developing Leaders*)

A consistent theme in Army doctrine is that skills are the metric of leader development. Leaders acquire, refine, and implement skills that allow them to accomplish tasks at increasing levels of responsibilities. **This association makes it easy for units to make training synonymous with leader development.**

Commanders implement programs that typically include classes, exercises, and events focusing on topics like warfighting doctrine, command supply discipline, career development, maintenance, the new OER/NCOER, and so on. In their messaging, they emphasize *"getting out to the range with your troops,"* conducting regular counseling, and doing good PT. These events fulfill the idea of leader development, which in reality is simply skill development.

Individuals need such skills to perform–fighting units must conduct these activities to succeed–but it's *leadership* that drives people to perform those tasks well, or at all. **Without strong leadership, the effectiveness of every other activity is compromised.**

Stuck in the Schoolhouse

Looking at the Army's leader development model from ADP 7-0, leader development occurs as Soldiers cycle through three domains: Institutional schooling teaches the fundamentals, operational assignments help leaders convert knowledge into practice, and self-development fills the gaps as a career progresses. In this model, training, education, and experience alternate as the primary means of development in each domain.

The problem is that today's Army culture views the study of leadership as "Education" and is quite comfortable letting the Institutional Domain teach it. Do we talk about the principles of leadership at the range or standing around in formation? No, we talk about them in the schoolhouse, where we spend a small portion of our careers. **We've come to believe that participation in unit training activities is sufficient to grow the leadership competencies of our Soldiers.**

This belief is inaccurate at best, as it is not uncommon to find that a good tactician is a bad leader—one may find recent case studies in the battalion and brigade commander firings of the last few years. But there is also a fundamental flaw in the belief that great leaders will naturally emerge from leader development programs comprised solely of unit training.

"It's on you, follower"

In a leader development program that excludes the study of leadership, responsibility for discerning the appropriate leadership lessons rests with the subordinates. Followers must have a desire to learn, be observant of their leaders, and know what leadership qualities to look for and internalize. All of this requires not only keen intuition, but the time and mental energy to do so while fulfilling the duties of their current position. This is a lot to ask of our subordinates.

To truly grow leaders instead of just skilled followers, leaders need to teach topics like example setting, self-development, learning from failure, building trust, having a success mindset, protecting the team, demanding the best performance, and so on. These aren't technical competencies, they're not warfighting competencies … they're leadership competencies. **If experienced leaders fail to make these lessons explicit during training and leader development events, they should not expect subordinates to model the behavior and become good leaders themselves.**

- Leader development means teaching the *How* and *Why*, while the team is doing the *What*.
- Leader development means elevating the conversation above the level of task execution.
- Leader development means talking about leadership on a daily basis, not just in the schoolhouse.
- **"Leader development" is incomplete without leadership.**

Putting Leadership Back in Leader Development

Take a look at your unit calendar. Scan the clutter of appointments, meetings, formations, training events, ceremonies, and administrative commitments. Do you see any events dedicated to improving the quality of your people's leadership? If not—if leadership development isn't a separate line of effort—then how are you developing leaders?

Where Did Leadership Go?

In the section "Have We Removed Leadership from Leader Development?," I asserted that the modern concept of military leader development largely overlooks the study of leadership. Discourse on leadership chiefly occurs in the schoolhouses of the professional military education system then takes a backseat to experience and training in operational units. When units "Develop leaders in everything they do," leader development becomes synonymous with training, where skills are the key metric of individual progress. Simply "getting out with the troops" fulfills the requirement to develop them, regardless of the discussions that occur. Finally, this relationship puts the burden of discerning what constitutes leadership lessons onto the subordinate instead of onto the leader.

Today's unit leaders are experiencing this dynamic. The study of leadership is either totally absent from unit leader development programs or is last on the priority list. Technical competencies, staff processes, unit administrivia, the study of doctrine, and so on all earn spots on the unit calendar ahead of a lecture, exercise, or discussion on leadership.

And so, a question emerges. Does this environment prevent our leaders from growing to their full potential? If you believe it does, like I do, then we are called to answer a second question: In what ways can we modify our concept of leader development to ensure that our peoples' leadership competencies are elevated along with other competencies?

The Challenge of Building Leaders

By coincidence, I began rereading *The Challenge of Command*, Roger Nye's exceptional analysis of command. In it I found a strikingly relevant model that provides a framework for this discussion. Nye cites military historian I.B. Holley of Duke University in presenting "Four Learning Objectives for Commanders." The model gives a baseline from which we can sort and analyze leader development activities.

Nye states that, "skilled learners pursue four objectives in any learning exercise they undertake":

1. *Knowledge.* Information, data, facts, theories, concepts. Answers question: "What should I know?" May be achieved by many learning methods. Highly perishable.
2. *Skills.* Abilities that can be developed and manifested in performance, not merely in potential. Answers question: "What should I be able to do?" Includes technical, communications, information-retrieval, and some analytical skills.
3. *Insights.* Ideas and thoughts derived internally from an ability to see and understand clearly the nature of things. Necessary part of making judgments, of deciding, of "putting it all together," of "being aware" of wisdom, far-sightedness. Answers questions: "What does this mean? What is important in this situation?" Cannot be taught directly, but can be induced by qualified teachers. Generally a product of education rather than training.
4. *Values.* Convictions, fundamental beliefs, standards governing the behavior of people. Includes attitudes towards professional standards such as duty, integrity, loyalty, patriotism, public service, and phrases such as "take care of your people" and "accomplish your missions." Answers questions: "What do I believe? Where

do I draw the line?" Values, like insights must be derived by the individuals, if they are to have meaning.

This list progresses from the hands-on, trainable activities of Knowledge and Skills, to the cognitive-based activities of Insights and Values. Knowledge and Skills encompass the abilities that people must bring to bear on a problem, while Insights and Values deal with how learners apply those abilities to achieve effects. Substitute the word "leaders" for "skilled learners," and this chart becomes an effective framework for analyzing leader development.

Without intention, unit leader development programs will tend to gravitate towards Knowledge and Skills and incorporate Insights and Values much less frequently. Development at the individual, team, and squad levels will naturally focus on Skills, but even company and battalion level commands can overlook Insights and Values development when faced with a busy calendar.

While my first thought was to place the study of leadership into the Values category, I instead believe it exists outside of this framework. ADP 6-22 says that leadership is a developable skill, but it is a misnomer to say that learning leadership is like learning to drive or put a weapon into operation. **Because leadership is based on influencing people, nothing about it involves muscle memory.** Leadership is situational, emotional, and effects based. In a reciprocal fashion, it actually draws on the Knowledge, Skills, Insights, and Values the leader has internalized, and at the same time uses those components to exert influence.

Transitioning to Leadership Development

It is these principles that are often absent as we develop our leaders. While there are no "steps" to follow to become an effective leader, there are countless leadership principles that can form a foundation of study. And only imagination limits leaders from integrating those lessons into unit activity.

Here are a few thoughts to consider as you strive to put leadership at the core of leader development.

—Recognize leadership as a standalone subject and dive into it!

Walk into Barnes & Noble and you'll see that leadership is a thriving genre that takes many forms. Sections on management, entrepreneurship, organizational development, personality types, and even self-help all contain useful perspectives from which military leaders can learn. Of course, the military history section contains relevant content, but there is great value to be found when leaders step outside of their comfort genre and generate insight inspired from parallel professions.

I would not be the leader I am today without the literary help of John Maxwell, Stephen Covey, Peter Drucker, Jim Collins, John Wooden, Marshall Goldsmith, Robert Sutton, Dave Ramsey, Malcolm Gladwell, and many others. As I read their perspectives on leadership, I made connections that worked their way into my own leading years later. Lately, podcasts and blogs have had a similar influence through the likes of Michael Hyatt, Andy Stanley, Seth Godin, and my friends in the Military Writers Guild.

Over the years, I've noticed several benefits that come from engaging in a personal program of leadership research. The same can happen for you. Diving into leadership will:

- Offer context (and sometimes answers) to leadership challenges you're facing
- Provide useful material to quote or disseminate to your teams
- Invite you to view the world through a lens of leadership, noting opportunities as well as problems you might have otherwise missed

Because leadership is a part of everything we do, a self-development program of leadership can easily become a program for team development. When you think about it, if leadership by example is a trait worth pursuing, leaders must become students of leadership if they are to develop leaders themselves.

—Integrate leadership into leading.

Leader development without a discussion of leadership is just skill development. It is possible to go to the rifle range and not learn anything about leadership, but why miss the opportunity to teach subordinates how to lead Soldiers in the execution of that range? It is possible to hold a battalion operations order briefing and not learn anything about the commander's decision making. But what better place to expose the experience and insight of the unit's most seasoned leader?

Leaders can put leadership back into leader development by simply conveying the *How* and the *Why* in the midst of conducting the *What*. Set the example, then *talk* about setting the example. Take responsibility for your actions, then *explain* why that's important. Demand excellence, then *show* your subordinates how to do it in an inspirational way. Lead, then *teach* others how to lead. Doing so takes the guesswork out of followership and makes subordinates feel like they're actually growing instead of just executing. Real impact occurs when that shift happens.

It's also time for leaders to elevate the quality of their conversations. Knowledge and Skills enable subordinates to do their jobs, but it is Insights and Values that really change them. What do you talk about during the idle time of military life? Do you make the effort to spark excitement about military service, about leadership? Do you challenge people away from their comfort zone with language that inspires growth?

If you're using words like integrity, honor, influence, loyalty, discipline, character, respect, initiative, fairness, responsibility, clarity, excellence, growth, reward, failure, example, emotion, passion, ethics, perseverance, trust, expectation, duty, vision, effectiveness, inspiration, and humility, then you're on the right track. This is the language of leadership.

—Dedicate unit time to leadership.
I'll conclude this section where it began, with the calendar. If it's not on the calendar, it's not a priority and it's not happening. It is the leader's responsibility to not only make leader development a priority, but also to shape the environment to allow its implementation.

For instance, counseling must have its own block time, perhaps an entire day per month. Subordinates must have support in attending schools that give them the needed skills to advance. And if leadership is not a routine topic of conversation, then dedicate the opening ten minutes of every meeting to sharing lessons of the week, watching a TED talk, or doing a "round the horn" of favorite quotes. Get the team out of their offices and into the auditorium to hear from a war hero, prominent local leader, or sports figure. Subordinates will know that leadership is a priority because they'll be engaged in it.

Grow Yourself … Grow Your Leaders

In many units today, leader development has become skill development. Activities that illuminate the art of leadership are seldom seen on a calendar saturated with training, staff processes, and organizational demands. Unfortunately, the quality of those very events diminishes if leadership competencies do not progress.

The goal of this and the previous section is to motivate leaders to make leadership a core part of their leader development programs and daily engagement. It's as simple as asking a thought-provoking question or explaining why you lead the way you do. Our subordinates want to be better leaders, not just competent followers.

The Bee, the Brain, & the Bully

Leadership is as diverse as the individuals who exercise it. We influence through distinct talents, shaped by experiences, personality traits, core values, and an endless list of other factors. Nonetheless, when we look back at the leaders we've encountered, it's easy to identify behavior trends that point to a set of defining leadership styles. The aggressive risk taker. The deliberate planner. The encouraging coach. The intense micromanager.

Each profession has its own set of styles that generally lead to success. The military is no different. Here are three types of military leaders you'll find that, for better or worse, produce results.

"The Bee"

The Bee is the leader who is in the office at 0400, leaves at 2100, and leads at 110 mph while he's there. **He's an overachiever who drives the organization through sheer force of will.** In organizational leadership terms, The Bee is known as a _pacesetter_.

If in a significant leadership position like command, The Bee will dart from meeting to meeting, range to range, subordinate command to subordinate command, engaging with troops and giving rapid-fire guidance. If in a staff position, The Bee will spend most of the day furiously creating products, tweaking PowerPoint slides, and slinging out emails in a mad rush to meet the flood of tasks with an equally opposing level of staff activity.

You may find that The Bee is an extrovert, motivated and energized by the high number of people he can visit with and coach every day. **The Bee will**

often sacrifice personal comfort to maintain his pace of leadership. He'll forget to eat, sleep too little, and may end up cranky because of it. The Bees I've seen in my career, though, are physically fit because they approach fitness with as much vigor as they do leading.

One problem with The Bee is that he sees his time in the leadership position as a sprint, while the rest of the team sees a marathon. As the commander, he may run at 110 mph but the staff only runs at 80. This disconnect will always be frustrating for The Bee. Reality will never match up to the high-paced vision he has for the organization.

In the end, The Bee is a positive leader who influences through motivation and constant growth. He spreads this attitude around the formation and inspires people to do more and become more than they thought possible. Higher commanders recognize this effect and appreciate not only that The Bee is accomplishing the mission, but that he is building a motivated team in the process.

"The Brain"

The Brain leads through intellect. **She thinks about success in terms of process-refinement and builds highly functioning teams by solving problems and removing obstacles.** The Brain is the smartest person in the room but doesn't hold it over her people's heads. She leads by asking challenging questions, inventing creative solutions, and spending time to educate and coach subordinates.

The Brain will challenge your assumptions and ask you to back up your recommendations with facts. She remembers and often references doctrine as a baseline standard for performance. When asked a question, The Brain will think first, then speak.

The Brain usually has lots of feedback for the group and can tell you how to do your job before you even start thinking about it. This can be good and bad. Good, because The Brain comes up with insight that your inexperience prevents you from seeing. Bad, because you don't get to learn the lesson on your own. The Brain really resonates with followers who learn by observing. But for those who learn by doing, The Brain can be frustrating because her poignant questions and good ideas often prevent people from learning through failure.

Whereas The Bee focuses on the activity at hand, The Brain considers how all the unit activity fits together to achieve the mission. The Bee gets antsy in meetings; The Brain does not. The Brain will read the operations order and all the annexes; The Bee will likely not. The Brain needs to prioritize her personal calendar and plan the day; The Bee will jump right in and not look up until the day is over.

Higher commanders love The Brain because she gives exceptional counsel. She is a confidante who puts things in perspective. You'll find The Brain attending advanced schooling and excelling in Commander's Initiatives Groups.

Sometimes a leader will exhibit the best aspects of both The Bee and The Brain. We call these leaders superstars. They can do it all. And you'll often see leaders transition from Bee to Brain as they move from the hands-on tactical leadership of the lower ranks to the systems-oriented landscape of the higher ranks.

Finally, it's important to note that The Bee and The Brain both possess a key personality trait which prevents them from digressing into this third type of leader.

"The Bully"

Just like The Bee and The Brain, The Bully gets the mission done (otherwise he'd never climb the ranks). **The Bully just gets it done at the expense of his followers, leaving them personally worse off.** You'll commonly see The Bully display the work ethic of The Bee. He's an overachiever but fails to notice when he's destroying people and teams. He sees his own activity in competition with his team's work and is afraid his followers will outshine him.

The Bully relies heavily on experience over logic and fails to capitalize on the formation's potential. What results is a high-paced, "directed course of action" leadership environment. When capable subordinates try to tell

The Bully that the team is stretched too thin to implement his latest good idea, The Bully barks, "Get it done, anyway!"

The Bully feels the same tension that The Bee feels when the team isn't sprinting as fast as he is. What The Bully can't understand is that the team will *never* reach that pace. Consequently, he berates and belittles them.

There are three reasons Bullies continue to get promoted: First, Bullies drive organizations to produce (though they take all the credit when talking to outsiders). Second, their higher leaders are too busy to investigate what is really going on in The Bully's formation, seeing only the results. (A boss of mine once said, "You can fool your boss, but you can't fool your peers or subordinates.") Third, ranking Bullies see themselves in others and promote the behavior.

The Key Difference

Here's what separates The Bee and The Brain from The Bully. They have emotional intelligence which allows them to feel empathy for their people. They run fast and they outthink their people, but they can sense the limits of their formation's capability. Then they coach and mentor to close the gap. They ask for feedback and consider it when leading. Even in the midst of a hectic schedule, The Bee and The Brain stop to celebrate milestones and personal achievements. And they know their own success depends on how successful their people are, then highlight those successes to anyone who will listen.

What leadership type are you? Have you thought about it lately? Here are some questions to consider as you strive to be a little less Bully and a little more of anything else:

- What methods can I employ to discover what my people are really experiencing under my leadership?
- In what ways can I bring forth the talent of those around me?
- How can I create an environment that invites collaboration, creativity, and feedback?
- What triggers can I emplace to find out when the formation is stretched beyond capacity? How would I know?

- How can I maintain a personal connection despite my high pace of activity?
- How should I shape my performance evaluations to discover the Bullies in my formation?

— empathy

← does an evolving leader experience all of these at some time? is the goal to balance between the 3?

& this argues you should never be a bully... are there times where this could be a conscious choice?

12 Tips for Effectively Counseling Your Subordinates

Counseling your team is a lot like creating a leader development program: *If you overthink it, it'll never get done.* Plenty of leaders groan when we talk about counseling and typically cite any of the following reasons for not getting it done:

"It takes so much time to counsel everyone each month."
"I give plenty of feedback in meetings and other times."
"My people already know where they stand."
"We have more pressing priorities than counseling. You know we're deploying, right?"

But most often, leaders don't counsel because they're uncomfortable with giving direct feedback. They also have difficulty telling subordinates that they're doing an average job (it's the best and the worst performers that are the easiest to give feedback to).

Leaders have to overcome these objections.

Not only is formal feedback required in almost every organization, but the process brings incredible value to your team. Your subordinates *want* to hear how they are doing. They *want* to get better. They *want* to learn from you. The key to successful counseling is to make the sessions interesting and worth their (and your) time.

Here are several tips that leaders can use to make counseling more effective and more likely to happen:

- **Just do it!** As with most tasks that we're uncomfortable with or have little experience doing, just getting a few reps in will break down apprehension and inject confidence about the process.

- **Simplify the method.** There's no need to fill out an elaborate feedback form prior to every counseling session. I had a commander who used a simple format on a single-page Word document with the headings: Strengths, Weaknesses, Way-Ahead. It was easy and effective.

- **Record feedback notes as they occur.** Don't wait until the morning of the counseling session to write your assessment of the subordinate. Doing so is unfair because you'll undoubtedly forget a lot of the good and the bad. Keep an easily-accessible digital document or a notepad handy to record feedback points for later.

- **Get out of the office and find an alternate venue.** No one likes the awkward, one-on-one scenario that feels scripted and formal. Do your counseling during a workout or over breakfast, where you have an activity to break up the conversation and facilitate engagement.

- **Block off time for counseling.** If counseling is important, schedule it on the unit calendar so that your subordinate leaders actually have the time to do it.

- **Tailor your sessions.** Ask what type of counseling is most effective for each subordinate and accommodate within reason.

- Open the counseling by having your subordinate review what he's been working on and **assess her own performance.** This allows her to bring up anything you might not have observed and gives you a perspective of her challenges and priorities.

- **"Don't step around the unsaid."** Few worthwhile lessons ever come from comfortable conversations. Get uncomfortable about why the subordinate made certain decisions. If there was failure, unpack the scenario to draw out the best lessons. If the follower is struggling with an issue (professional or personal), redirect the conversation to uncover the root cause and help them solve it.

- **Involve them in the process.** Make your team feel comfortable about telling you their successes and failures. There are lots of commendable actions that go on beneath your radar. Encourage them to send you a quick note when something goes well and to include you in challenges they're facing.

- **Set performance standards and over-communicate them.** There's nothing worse than going into a feedback session thinking you're doing well, only to find out that you've been missing the mark for some time. This scenario is incredibly unfair and corrosive. Especially in an era of a downsizing military, publish your standards of performance and emphasize them at every opportunity. Your approach should include something that sounds like, "Not all of you will be rated in the top tier, but if you want to perform your way into the top tier, you need to ..."

- **Bookend with positives.** Unless you're giving feedback to the bottom 10%, everyone on your team wants to do the right thing and perform well. Acknowledge that fact and accentuate the positive. You want your subordinates to leave the meeting with the motivation to work on the improvement areas, not feel dejected and hopeless about them.

- **Find teachable moments.** Don't wait for a scheduled counseling session if there is a clear opportunity to give good feedback and teach a lesson. Your team will appreciate this and your feedback is more likely to stick because it's being received in the emotional and situational context of the event.

clear intentional communication

think before you deliver

Leaders, Your Facebook Phobia is Holding You Back

Let's start off by coming to an agreement that your Facebook feed probably looks like most people's—vacation photos, social quizzes, kitten videos, weddings, parties, and babies. You might post a few thoughts about the latest political buzz, but you're not writing to change anyone's opinion or move them in a new direction. Facebook is a window to the *social* You, not the *professional* You.

Am I right?

Now a question: Where is your largest connected network? Is it at your workplace? Your gym? Through your family? Or is it through Facebook?

If you're not in the business of influence, then this discussion is irrelevant. But if you are a leader, then it's worthwhile to consider how you use your most expansive network. If you care about changing people in positive ways, then you need to rethink Facebook.

The Obstacles

When it comes to Facebook, I've heard leaders cite a number of reasons for not using it for professional influence. Do any of these sound familiar?

- "I don't want to 'friend' the people I work with."
- "In the military, it's fraternization to connect with subordinates on social media."

- "I don't want my work colleagues to see my personal posts."
- "There's no good professional content to share."
- "I don't have time to spend on Facebook."
- "My friends and family don't want to see professional posts in their feeds."
- "My team will think I want to snoop on them if I ask to connect on Facebook."
- "My unit already has a leader development program, so I don't need any other methods."

And if it's not because of a specific reason like these, a lot of people have simply **never viewed Facebook as a medium for anything other than family photos.**

Weapon of Mass Influence

I can devote a paragraph to discrediting each of the claims above, but I'll summarize by saying that they are minor obstacles standing in the way of an opportunity to have significant positive impact. It is outdated nonsense to believe that becoming Facebook friends with coworkers and subordinates is inappropriate. **Facebook is a digital connection, not a date.** And the privacy settings are so easily adjustable that leaders can tailor their feeds and posts to target specific groups, thus avoiding the concerns about personal information.

The other false assumption worth mentioning is that people don't want to see personal or professional development content on Facebook. Again, people can use privacy settings as a filter, but **since when do great leaders go silent because they think people don't want to be led?** I promise you that your network is just like you: They'll be happy to gain inspiration, insight, and development whenever and wherever they can get it.

Like and Share

If you are a leader, you have the responsibility to be a content producer, not just a content consumer. There is a massive amount of valuable professional content going out on Facebook and other social media platforms. You wouldn't hesitate to pass on a good leadership lesson from your boss. Similarly, **don't let good professional content stop with you**, wherever it's posted.

Make a difference through social media in just a few steps:

- Start intentionally building your influence network by 'friending' coworkers, teammates, and anyone else you think would benefit from content that matters.
- Adjust your privacy settings to tailor your own feed, as well as how you distribute content.
- Start following the sites that will grow you and your team (military blogs, official pages, defense commentary, etc.).
- Share the relevant content and add your own comments so your people know how it applies to them.
- Use the material as a primer for professional discussions at work.

Today, there is no more expansive digital network than Facebook. Leaders who care about developing people will use every possible avenue to make a difference, which means overcoming our fear of using it to develop our people and teams.

The Most Important Leadership Quote You'll Read this Year

When I read this leadership quote a few weeks ago, I kicked myself for not having found it sooner. (It's the type of advice I'd put in my signature block ... and I'm not even a "signature block philosophy" kind of emailer.) It is attributed to the immutably inspirational leader of the Allied coalition in World War II, General Dwight D. Eisenhower. This insight is powerful because it captures the fundamental nature, the heart, of what it means to be a leader. And Eisenhower uses only 26 words to do it.

Here is what I read from General Dwight D. Eisenhower:

> *"Soldiers will not follow any battle leader with confidence unless they know that he will require full performance of duty from every member of the team."*

You may want to read it again. If the universal impact of Eisenhower's counsel doesn't sink in right away, permit me to offer my thoughts on why this quote should adorn the cover of every leader's notebook.

Fundamental Truth

From highly specific situational guidance to hopelessly abstract theoretical nonsense, leadership advice has a broad spectrum. One can fill a bookshelf with the tomes dedicated to simply defining it. There exist, however, what I like to think of as core tenets of leadership, the themes that transcend situational particulars and apply to every leadership environment. One might call them Principles of Leadership. *"Leaders must lead by example,"* is certainly one. John Maxwell's, *"Everything rises and falls on leadership,"* is one that I consider core. Powell's *"Leadership is solving problems,"* might be another. Eisenhower's wisdom is undoubtedly among these universal principles.

He specifies "battle" leader, but the idea is certainly not limited to that setting. Instead, it relates to every moment of a leader's duty day. Combat may offer intrinsic motivation for all to perform at their best, but success in garrison also requires inspirational leadership, perhaps even more so because in battle the cost of failure is plainly evident.

This advice is fundamental because **demanding the best out of the team is the only way to accomplish the mission.** (What team ever found victory by giving their worst?) Legendary UCLA coach John Wooden led with the mindset that success would only be found by extracting the absolute best from every individual on the team. When individuals performed their best, the team would be poised to win. That is the essence of leadership.

Commitment to Excellence

Imagine hearing Eisenhower's statement from your leader. Doesn't it carry with it the promise that the entire team is committed to excellence? I would take great satisfaction in knowing that my leader's goal is to hold everyone accountable to "full performance of duty." Note also that "every member of the team" includes the leader! This statement is a 360 degree promise, a two-way street, a pact to give 100% to the mission. That's the team I want to be a part of.

What follows from that realization is the only thing that keeps teams together ... trust. When the team members know each other will perform to standard, including the leader, trust has fertile soil to grow. Realize also, that when the opposite occurs—when leaders don't hold team members to the full performance of duty—then no one will trust the leader. Thus, **trust can only develop when leaders hold teams accountable to achieve excellence.**

Setting the Standard

There's one more aspect of Eisenhower's quote that struck me. As any military leader will confess, counseling is a commonly overlooked practice. Too many subordinates execute their daily tasks without ever receiving clear standards of performance, then are disheartened to discover an underwhelming evaluation report at the end of the year. I believe this happens because leaders fail to define what success looks like. Likewise, they don't explain what practices and behaviors subordinates must avoid to prevent failure.

If leaders would simply set clear standards, they would find performance counseling much easier. Eisenhower's counsel demands this. For leaders to *require full performance of duty from every member of the team*, they must clarify performance expectations **and** provide regular feedback. This is the most effective way to gain confidence among followers.

Demanding Leadership

General Eisenhower's statement makes it clear: **Demand the best from the entire team and you'll inspire their best while gaining their trust.** If his leadership quote isn't on the cover of your green notebook, what is? What are you doing to inspire the best leadership you can offer your team? This advice, from arguably the most influential general in American history, is a good place to start.

Leadership Speed and Why It Matters

Earlier, in "How Do You Spot a Leader?", I shared some of the guidance I issued during my company command time years ago. I suggested the notion that leaders naturally move faster than everyone else.

If you are a leader and you find yourself moving slowly throughout the day, you are probably not doing enough to help out the team. Most of the time, leaders dart from one event to the next, or are focusing to create a new product/presentation that will help the team. They are always looking to identify problems in the organization and tackle them quickly, so that the organization can become better or more effective.

Leaders create and disseminate energy throughout the organization to keep it moving in the right direction and responding appropriately to the environment. There is an inherent risk, however, for naturally driven leaders who move quickly towards success.

The Reverse Pony Express

I once heard a friend draw a comparison between "individual speed" and "team speed." I don't think he had given the terms much thought, but simply used them to label the disconnect that occurs when a leader moves at a pace the team cannot follow.

We see this consistently in purpose-driven, competitive organizations like the military. Passionate men and women prepare for years to assume the mantle of leadership, yet fail to recognize that their subordinates:

- Don't share their personal drive for success
- Don't have the same level of experience or training
- Don't have the same access to information, nor the same organizational perspective as the leader
- Cannot avoid the fact that they are on a team with *other people*, which inherently moves slower than the leader (maybe because they're the ones actually *doing* the work?)

New leadership comes in and works the team into the ground. It's the reverse Pony Express effect: **Instead of keeping the same rider and swapping the horse to preserve its longevity, we put a fresh rider in the saddle and expect the exhausted horse to keep on running.**

What is Your Leadership Speed?

I use the phrase *leadership speed* to describe this notion of competing speeds of organizational activity. Take a quick look at your organization and you'll quickly see natural divisions in capability which will result in friction. I mentioned the new leader with an old team, but think about how staff sections function at different paces, or the varying responsiveness that subordinate units will show as a result of competing priorities.

Leaders need to recognize that any number of factors influence how effectively the team will be able to keep up with them. Those who ignore this concept, risk not only running their teams into the ground, but also failing to meet priorities. They must also come to the realization that **not every activity needs to occur at full throttle.** However, it usually takes a closed-door session or an organizational breakdown for that realization to sink in.

Dismount and Discover

Here are a few thoughts to help you get out of the saddle and make sure you're riding at a pace your horse can actually sustain:

- **Accept.** You need to start by admitting that not everyone is as good as you are and that the team can't instantly achieve the big ideas you come up with. Behind every one of your statements of guidance is a mound of actual work that takes time, energy, talent, patience, and your protection from distraction. **Accept that your pony can't run as fast as you wish it could.**

- **Analyze.** Grab a white board, bring in your advisors, and figure out where the team isn't meeting your expectations. What factors influence that outcome? Are they undertrained? Are they the wrong people for the job? Do they lack resources? How could you have better enabled them for success? Or is it possible you have a distorted or misinformed understanding of their work situation?

- **Ask.** Leaders routinely fail to see the power in simply asking for feedback. There's nothing wrong with asking your teammates and subordinates: *Am I pushing the team too hard? What is your section struggling with? Do you have enough time and resources to meet my intent? Do you feel our priorities are appropriate? Does my daily guidance align with those priorities? If you were in my shoes for a day, what would you change?* Go ahead, ask and let them speak. What you'll find is that instead of weakening your position as a leader, **you'll gain enormous respect** because your team will feel included, empowered, and enthusiastic about becoming a more effective organization … provided you lead them to be so.

- **Adjust.** Finally, it's time to refine your leadership speed. Scrutinize your priorities and guidance and admit that everything can't be the most important thing. Consider what will have to come off the plate if you do X. Review your good ideas to see if they're the *right* ideas. Ponder for a moment the vast difference in capability that you've gained in your career compared to those you lead. What are you expecting of them that they just haven't learned yet? **Where could you improve effectiveness by teaching instead of scrutinizing?** Then, as you close the gap between "individual speed" and "team speed," remember that shortcomings don't necessarily mean that your people are running too slowly, but that you might be running too fast.

Finding the Fine Line

I want to close by highlighting that leaders must also strive to find that fine line between "getting the most out of the team" and "pushing them too hard." Military leadership will forever require that leaders extract more out of their individuals and teams than they think they are capable of giving. **Leaders must push their units, for combat is the Kentucky Derby.** But it is also the leader's responsibility to ensure the horse arrives at the starting gate in top condition, not broken from stress and overtraining.

Why Do Toxic Leaders Keep Getting Promoted?

Becoming a successful leader should mean more than just getting the mission done. It should also mean taking care of Soldiers and families and making a difference in the lives of those we lead. We don't talk about it often, but that's what we intuitively feel. Followers desire leaders who guide the team to accomplish the mission while respecting and inspiring them.

And what's the common theme among toxic leaders who continue to ascend the ranks? They get the mission done but leave a trail of destruction in their wake. Bosses routinely fail to identify toxic subordinate commanders, but peers and subordinates always feel the impact. Why does this happen? Why do senior raters look down at subordinate leaders and see mission accomplishment but not the negative interactions they use to make it happen?

Reacting Instead of Initiating

Tom Rath, in *Strengths Based Leadership* (a book that I routinely recommend and reference), offers a passage that helps explain why mission accomplishment – by almost any means necessary – is so highly valued when it comes to leader performance:

> ... even the highest level executives reported that they spend almost all of their time *reacting* to the needs of the day instead of *initiating* for their future.

One challenge is that our ability to progress in our career is often determined by our effectiveness in responding to near-term needs. When high value is placed on solving these kinds of problems, it creates a culture in which leaders spend little or no time thinking about what *could* be done because they receive more accolades for simply doing what *needs* to be done.

Another reason we get caught in perpetual response mode is because it's easier. Agreeing to take on a small objective – for example, cleaning out your inbox by the end of each day – is much more manageable than embarking on a larger and more proactive goal – like creating a new product or mapping out how to double your business in three to five years. Solving problems and removing barriers comes naturally to many people, while initiating is much harder work.

Think about the military leader's day. In your experience, would you say that most time is spent *initiating* effort to grow the organization? Or is most of the day spent *reacting* to outside requirements and solving immediate crises? I think most would say the latter.

A Task-Saturated Culture

The problem is that most leaders live in a task-saturated environment, which impedes them from analyzing the effects of their actions and discourages them from seeking ways to reach their unit's or their own full potential. Time and again, I've seen junior officers and NCOs struggle to find the cognitive space, for example, to apply creativity to their training events or develop long-term leader development plans. **The endless supply of "5-meter targets" prevents leaders from being the guide their organizations need. And our culture rewards them for it.**

Senior raters end up recommending advancement for subordinate leaders who tackle the near-term targets because 1) the tasks are usually coming from the senior chain of command, which has a vested interest in seeing them accomplished, and 2) the effort is visible and easy to measure. *"How many on-time evaluations did A Company have?"* is a lot easier to assess and evaluate than *"Is the A Company Commander inspiring a culture of trust?"* And most leaders are more comfortable having a conversation about the timeliness of evaluations than they are about establishing trust in the organization.

When senior raters focus on the flurry of near-term subordinate activity, they risk overlooking the methods by which subordinate leaders achieve the mission. Too often, immediately behind the curtain of a "successful" leader is an egocentric environment of micromanagement and mistrust that overworks its members and fails to personally and professionally develop them.

Causes and Cures?

After stewing on this, I'm still left with questions that maybe you can consider, as well.

- Does a focus on near-term tasks lead to bad leadership?
- Are toxic leaders getting promoted simply because they get the mission done?
- What areas should senior raters prioritize when evaluating the quality of their subordinates' leadership environment?
- What methods can leaders use to build an environment of trust and development despite a full calendar and endless task list?

The Priceless Leadership
Insight of Robert Sutton

I want to highlight the outstanding work of Robert Sutton, who published "12 Things Good Bosses Believe" in Harvard Business Review and inspired my effort to bring the list into a military context. I immediately connected with his 12 Bosses advice and would put it in the hands of every military member if I could. Further, his books are exceptional deep dives into appropriate and effective leader behavior.

Many thanks to Bob for granting permission to utilize his ideas, both on The Military Leader website and in this book. Many people will benefit from his generosity.

12 Things Good Bosses Believe (#1)

"I have a flawed and incomplete understanding
of what it feels like to work for me."

Sutton points out the sociological fact that followers are hypersensitive to the leader's actions, watching for behaviors that indicate changes in their environment. Conversely, those in charge focus on themselves and tune-out subordinates.

The nature of command in the military exaggerates this principle. We have always held our commanders in the highest regard and Army Regulation 600-20 gives them absolute authority. Everything the Army does supports a commander and, within legal/moral/ethical boundaries, they have total power to change course or run the ship aground.

As such, it is easy for a commander to be the center of a unit's attention. There's an argument that says the commander SHOULD be the center of attention, because she's the one who will make the tough calls and the one who bears responsibility for the Soldier's welfare and ultimate survival. In combat, this is rational.

But in the day-to-day running of the unit, a commander can change the work environment for the positive (facilitating creativity; fostering participation/teamwork) by reducing his authoritative presence. This lets subordinate leaders take more responsibility and exposes team dynamics she might not otherwise see.

The Mission Command concept even encourages this type of leadership, where the leader sets his boundaries for the mission (his intent) and steps away to let the staff develop courses of action. We all know how painfully unproductive it is when the commander/leader hovers over a process, inserting course corrections and interrupting momentum.

Bottom Line

- Look for opportunities where your reduced presence might allow the team to flourish.
- Find ways to check the pulse of your organization and become more sensitive to the team's needs.
- Acknowledge that being a military leader gives you a lot of power, but you're still dealing with human beings who don't necessarily enjoy living in a world that revolves around you.

12 Things Good Bosses Believe (#2)

"My success — and that of my people — depends largely on
being the master of obvious and mundane things,
not on magical, obscure, or breakthrough ideas or methods."

Robert Sutton's second belief about good bosses reminds us that while it is important for leaders to create vision for the organization, the more important work deals with leading people through the tangible steps to achieve that vision.

Consider commanders you've seen that set out "Command Philosophies" containing lofty goals and the challenge to reach ill-defined levels of "*x*" capability. These documents may chart a path, but they're not what the junior leader will rely on when he's trying to do his part to reach those goals.

Our military typically operates in a complex environment during combat, and a muddled, overtasked environment in garrison. It is the leader's job to sort through the muck to clearly define the steps/systems the team must perform to reach his goal. Task – Purpose – Endstate. Teams need this clarity to perform well.

Also, consider that our system affords certain perks and comforts to commanders (his own vehicle, good accommodations, etc.) because it expects them to get their head out of the weeds and identify the "obvious" when the team is rowing too hard to see what's ahead.

12 Things Good Bosses Believe (#3)

"Having ambitious and well-defined goals is important, but it is useless to think about them much. My job is to focus on the small wins that enable my people to make a little progress every day."

More important than creating big goals is to actually connect those goals to each level in the organization.

This is the process of translating a Mission Statement into Commander's Intent into actionable tasks. ("There's the hill we're going to seize, but nevermind that because first we have to cross a minefield, and to do that I need you to mark the lane.")

It's vital for the team members to see that their small win contributes to the team's big win. And even though Soldiers will dutifully execute any task assigned them, leaders will shift from positional power to transformational power if they can connect at the Soldier level and show how their contribution matters.

12 Things Good Bosses Believe (#4)

"One of the most important, and most difficult, parts of my job
is to strike the delicate balance between being
too assertive and not assertive enough."

Fact: A team's performance decreases under too much pressure from its leadership.

It is also true that a team may underperform without enough pressure from the leader—but honestly, how often do you see under-motivated military leaders? Our challenge is usually in scaling back assertiveness and pressure so that our teams can perform their best.

Tommy Lasorda summarized it well: *"I believe managing is like holding a dove in your hand. If you hold it too tightly you kill it, but if you hold it too loosely, you lose it."*

Similarly, knowing WHEN to apply assertiveness is a skill of great leaders. They read the environment and anticipate when their teams will need pressure and when to back off. It's a common belief that military leaders must be constantly assertive, Type-A, and intense. But relying solely on that leadership approach can be counterproductive to achieving unit goals.

12 Things Good Bosses Believe (#5)

"My job is to serve as a human shield, to protect my people from
external intrusions, distractions, and idiocy of every stripe —
and to avoid imposing my own idiocy on them as well."

What a relevant rule for military organizations! How many times has your unit or your team been assigned some inconsequential task that prevented you from accomplishing your priority tasks? The challenge of balancing external influences and mission-focused activity is nothing new, and some would say impossible to perfect.

Nonetheless, good leaders believe they are a shield for their organization. They look for ways to safeguard their team from distraction and filter the mission-essential tasks from the administrivia. This frees the organization to focus and excel.

In what ways could you get a better sense of the intrusions and inefficiencies your people need protection from? Have you asked them what tasks and systems drag them down? Commanders have unique authority to cut through bureaucracy and red tape to force change. Actively look for ways to gain freedom to maneuver and help them stay laser-focused on what matters most.

12 Things Good Bosses Believe (#6)

"I strive to be confident enough to convince people that I am in charge, but humble enough to realize that I am often going to be wrong."

Item #6 of Robert Sutton's 12 Things Good Bosses Believe is one that should resonate with military leaders. Typically, we do not have difficulty convincing people that we are in charge; the long history of service and discipline inherently gives authority to leaders/commanders.

Still, exerting authority at the right time/place does not come naturally for some, so it may be necessary to look for opportunities to lead with intention and assertiveness. But let's be honest, most military leaders need to pay attention to the second half of Sutton's statement.

Being in charge doesn't mean you'll always be right. In fact, being a leader almost guarantees that your decisions will be wrong in at least some people's eyes. As General Colin Powell said, *"Leadership sometimes means making people mad."*

Sutton's point is that sometimes leaders will be flat-out wrong, and the good ones will be open-minded enough to sense it, be humble enough to admit it (publicly, if necessary), and be willing to listen to advice and correct the mistake.

12 Things Good Bosses Believe (#7)

> "I aim to fight as if I am right, and listen as if I am wrong —
> and to teach my people to do the same thing."

This should be a no-brainer. Military leaders generally don't have a problem fighting as if they're right, but what does "listen as if I am wrong" mean for leaders who are driven, experienced, and trained to perform with total confidence? Let's start by looking at the antithesis.

Here's what "listen as if I am wrong" DOESN'T MEAN:

- I talk through the entire engagement.
- I don't ask for feedback or opinions.
- I check my phone while others are explaining their points.
- I cram too many topics into a meeting, which prevents discussion time.
- I don't let the team know what I'm thinking.
- I only give intellectual or professional consideration to people in my "in" crowd.
- I assume I am the most talented person in the room.
- I don't foster open and unattributable discussion.

Have you experienced these before? See any trends? The leader is self-focused and assumes that no one else is going to offer anything of value, so he doesn't prioritize discussion or feedback. Followers easily pick up on that attitude and it immediately stifles their sense of inclusion and participation.

Here's what "listen as if I am wrong" might look like for a military leader:

- I allow and encourage the team to voice their opinions.
- I give undivided attention to whoever is speaking and I TAKE NOTES.
- I separate rank and position (including my own) from the discussion and place a premium on the content.
- I remain humble enough to brainstorm in front of my own team so they know my creative process.
- I ask questions that cause followers to expand and develop their ideas.
- I ask if there's a better way to accomplish the mission.
- I seek feedback to discover if my leadership style stifles participation and innovation.
- I give clear praise to those who get involved in the process and give tough feedback.

Sutton's Belief #7 highlights examples of how successful business leaders fostered this concept in their teams. One of those key concepts is that a leader should facilitate energetic discussion and ruthlessly honest feedback between members of the team, which typically leads to a fleshed-out idea with group buy-in.

12 Things Good Bosses Believe (#8)

"One of the best tests of my leadership — and my organization —
is "what happens after people make a mistake?"

Sutton explains that of his five books on business and leadership, #8 is the most important lesson:

Failure is inevitable, so the key to success is to be good at learning from it. The ability to capitalize on hard-won experience is a hallmark of the greatest organizations—the ones that are most adept at turning knowledge into action, that are best at developing and implementing creative ideas, that engage in evidence-based (rather than faith- or fear-based) management, and that are populated with the best bosses.

The military has a lineage of "no fail" leadership. There are clearly times when error, failure, or underperformance are unacceptable.

There are also times (I'm sure you can recall from your own experience) when military leaders have exercised "no-fail" leadership in situations that were slightly less decisive as D-Day. Unit meetings in garrison come to mind, where I've observed a commander routinely rip into the staff for minor (and often unavoidable) deviances from his perfect expectations. What is a person or team to do when they offer their best effort only to be cut down and reminded of their failings?

There are basically three responses to failure:

1. **Nobody notices.** In the military, not identifying failure is worse than overreacting to it. Given the importance of our military mission, this typically does not happen in the areas of warfighting. However, don't forget that "what doesn't get checked doesn't get done." It's easy to assume that areas like counseling and property management are "good to go" and not identify a problem until critical system failure.

2. **The team gets crushed.** In this case, the individual or team gives it their best but falls short and the leader gives no allowance for not meeting the standard. Sometimes a leader has to intentionally do so to make a point, but leading without allowance for failure destroys creativity, morale, and learning.

3. **The leader uses failure to grow the team.** Provided that failure wasn't illegal, immoral, or unethical, the leader should use every opportunity to calmly walk the individual/team through a process to objectively capture the facts, identify successes as well as faults, and then extrapolate the appropriate lessons. This leader assumes that everyone is doing their best and wants to learn. And when the leader couples this process with positive feedback for the parts that went well, the result is immeasurably productive.

The effects of having a measured response and using failure to grow will be twofold:

- **Productivity will increase.** The team members will feel inspired to seek excellence, won't be afraid of failure, and will be enabled to try new methods.
- **Trickle down effect.** Your subordinate leaders will follow the leader's example and treat their teams in a similar way, which elevates the entire organization's growth.

12 Things Good Bosses Believe (#9)

"Innovation is crucial to every team and organization.
So my job is to encourage my people to generate
and test all kinds of new ideas.
But it is also my job to help them kill off all the bad ideas
we generate, and most of the good ideas, too."

Sutton's Belief #9 from 12 Things Good Bosses Believe has significant, daily application for the military leader.

"Sure ... Yes! ... Absolutely!"

Innovation in the military is crucial, as it is in any industry. But we have a habit of saying YES to just about any idea that ultimately helps Soldiers. We have the tendency to support staff members and subordinate commanders who show enthusiasm for growth and are eager to make their mark on the organization. We let them try their pet ideas and "learn the lesson on their own," typically while exhausting resources and pulling the organization in too many directions. The result is often **mediocrity in lots of things instead of proficiency in the most important things.**

"No! ... Not a priority ... Thanks but it's not happening."

Because the military is a commander-centric model, staffs and subordinate commanders often won't/can't kill an idea without the boss's permission, which leads to stagnation, frustration, and wasted resources if the boss is not ruthlessly decisive.

Robert Sutton explains that leaders must execute a deliberate campaign to:

- **Find and kill** the organization's activities that are outdated or came from bad ideas to begin with
- **Block the bad ideas** – those that are not in line with the organization's priorities
- **Refine the good ideas** that are not the best ideas
- **Focus on best ideas** – the ones that achieve effects that are precisely in line with the organization's priorities

How do you know when you're starting to prioritize effectively? When people start complaining that there is no room on the calendar for their good ideas. At that point, it's important to give guidance on how to refine the idea or let it go. Sutton says, "The very best bosses teach and inspire their people to accept defeat gracefully and move forward to implement the selected ideas, even if none of their pet ideas made the cut."

Arguably, we have to be good at combat, and we have to be good at taking care of Soldiers and families. All else is bonus.

12 Things Good Bosses Believe (#10)

"Bad is stronger than good. It is more important to
eliminate the negative than to accentuate the positive."

In my first few weeks as a company commander, I noticed that directly across the hall worked a consistently loud mid-level leader. He made a point to interrupt and talk over everyone around him who was either junior in rank or wasn't annoyed enough to walk away.

As his leader, though, what concerned me was that his talk was also constantly negative. He seemed to be incapable of agreeing with or encouraging a positive thought from those around him. It was an emotional drain to listen to and I'm sure it was exasperating for the Soldiers working for him.

Belief #10 on Robert Sutton's 12 Things Good Bosses Believe zeros-in on negative interactions and caustic team members because they can quickly overwhelm the positive that exists within an organization. Being a nice leader and encouraging others is not enough.

Eliminating the negative, as any skilled leader can tell you, is not just the flipside of accentuating the positive. It's an entirely different set of activities. For someone with people to manage, accentuating the positive means recognizing productive and constructive effort, for example, and helping people discover and build on their strengths. Eliminating the negative, for the same boss, might mean tearing down maddening obstacles and shielding people from abuse.

Some might say that the climate of authority and bravado in military units makes positivity "uncool." Success in the military, like anything else, "rises and falls on leadership" (John Maxwell). Sutton's point is that actively developing a positive climate is less important than removing the negative people and interactions. Sutton draws an analogy to marriage:

> Negative information, experiences, and people have far deeper impacts than positive ones. In the context of romantic relationships and marriages, for example, the truth is stark: unless positive interactions outnumber negative interactions by five to one, odds are that the relationship will fail.

In the instance of my former subordinate, it was clear to me that his corrosive attitude was exactly the opposite of the command climate my First Sergeant and I were trying to build. One day after a particularly cynical monologue, I engaged him with an ultimatum: Cut out the negativity or I'd pull him out of the position, period. He adjusted his attitude.

Here are a few tips for action:

- Lead with positivity and publicly reward such behavior in your team.
- Words matter. Pay close attention to how you discuss problems and difficult people. Your attitude will propagate throughout the organization.
- Frame conflict in the context of growth, always placing the outcome and the learning process higher than the friction that caused it.
- Establish no tolerance for caustic, negative people.
- Go on the hunt for negative people. Roam around the building, get conversational, and investigate rumors of negative behavior.
- Use Baird CEO Paul Purcell's approach to clarify your stance on negativity: "If I discover that you're a [jerk], I'm going to fire you."

12 Things Good Bosses Believe (#11)

"*How* I do things is as important as what I do."

Simplicity resonates from Belief #11 of Robert Sutton's 12 Things Good Bosses Believe. This belief is so basic that it is often overlooked and rarely discussed, but might very well be the belief that distinguishes great leaders from the rest.

Consider #11 in light of the leaders you've observed. I have found that:

- **Average leaders** think their work is finished after making a decision; **great leaders** know that the hard part is execution and, as Benjamin Franklin quipped, "*Well done is better than well said.*"
- **Average leaders** let others figure out how to do the tedious tasks; **great leaders** use their experience to provide solutions for their team, even though the problems are beneath them.
- **Average leaders** think their authority will be the force that pushes the task along; **great leaders** use engagement, motivation, encouragement, vision, and example to lead their team in execution.
- **Great leaders** know that the *What* tells what occurred but the *How* tells the story that people will remember.
- **Great leaders** understand that the *How* is the personality of one's leadership. It's what will convince people to follow because they want to, not because they have to.

The *How* is crucial because it's how leaders achieve effect with their actions. The *What* is rarely enough.

For example, think about a battalion commander and command sergeant major who want to ensure their subordinate leaders are properly counseling Soldiers. The simplest *What* would be to just tell them to do it. The commander could also task the staff to develop and emplace a counseling program that creates a standard and verifies completion. This would be a better *How*.

But to achieve the effect of engaged leadership, thorough risk management, and systemic change, the battalion leaders would also do things like:

- Get personally involved in crafting the program
- Personally pitch the concept to the team to show it's a priority
- Include professional counseling education to enable the subordinate leaders
- Dedicate calendar time for units to conduct counseling
- Visit subordinate units and observe counseling sessions
- Formally evaluate subordinates on their ability to execute the program

Leaders achieve results when they accompany the *What* with a good *How*.

12 Things Good Bosses Believe (#12)

"Because I wield power over others,
I am at great risk of acting like an insensitive jerk — and not realizing it."

Robert Sutton closes out *12 Things Good Bosses Believe* by citing what I think is the most often overlooked (and potentially the most destructive) aspect of leadership on this list. It is the idea that **the very position of influence blinds the leader from truly realizing how his actions impact subordinates.**

When you think about it, there is nothing more elemental in human interaction—*to understand how we affect other people*—but this awareness is often hidden even from those who base their professions on influencing others.

Power and Insensitivity in Military Leadership

The significance of Sutton's statement is evident when you look at how its components relate to the military:

- **Power.** The severity of combat operations demands that *military leaders must be able to leverage near-absolute power in moments of crisis.* Power is built into the organization by the nature of command authority, through the legal obligations of the Uniform Code of Military Justice, and by the military's values and traditions.
- **Risk.** Leadership failure in the military can carry dire consequences, not just in combat but also in civil–military relations, public

scrutiny, and social trust. The military's recent struggle with toxic leadership exhibits that fact.

- **Insensitivity**. The very core of military leadership contains a healthy bit of stoic insensitivity– the notion that the commander is detached, unflappable, and immune to emotional stress.

So, the military gives its leaders a lot of power and partly relies on their insensitivity to lead in tough times. But we can all acknowledge that those times of crisis are few, and the majority of leadership time is spent navigating day-to-day routines, preparing for big events, tackling projects, managing systems, and running meetings.

Tips for Not Being a Jerk Boss

How can military leaders accept Sutton's 12th Belief about good bosses and ensure their own behavior doesn't negatively impact the organization? Here are a few tips:

- **Ask for feedback**. The best leaders ask for input from everyone around them because they realize their own perception is skewed by position and power. Provide formal and informal means to find out how your actions are affecting the individuals and the organization as a whole. You might be surprised.
- **Establish a "No-Jerk Rule" ... for yourself**. Robert Sutton's most popular book is devoted to this concept. Announce to your organization that jerks will not be tolerated. Then if you want to show them you're serious, give them permission to call you out if *you're the one being a jerk*.
- **Recognize the common good**. In the competitive environment of the military ranks, it's easy to brush off other people as less-talented or less-experienced. This is particularly true if you're the commander, the one who is expected to be the standard-bearer. But there's no reason to wield this power over your people or look down on them. The truth is that **most people really are doing their best to succeed**. If they fall short, it's probably due to lack of experience, or a lack of training, in which case it's the leader's fault.
- **Don't step on enthusiasm**. In the same vein, don't belittle people who show enthusiasm and heart, even if it's for an idea that

ultimately won't work or doesn't make sense. Redirect them gently, with encouragement. Appreciate the fact that you've got a worker who has the intellect, energy, and confidence to present an idea.

- **Praise the effort, not just the result**. Because the "suck it up" attitude is prevalent in our military, it's acceptable for staffs and subordinates to pour their heart, souls, time, and energy into a project, only to be judged solely on results. Yes, at the end of the day, we must achieve the military mission ... but that doesn't mean we can't be proud of and acknowledge all that it took to get there. **Praise your people along the journey, even if the road doesn't lead to absolute success**.

- **Ask personal questions**. I had the unfortunate experience of working with a boss who sat 8 feet from me for almost a year but never engaged me with a single personal question. He didn't care. Regardless of what his true intent was, to me he was an insensitive jerk. Your people want to know that you see more about them than just their work.

- **Be humble**. As I mentioned earlier, I once watched a Colonel get promoted to Brigadier General and as the three-star boss emplaced the new star on his uniform, he warned, *"Don't forget that this rank is held on by Velcro."* He said this partly to remind the officer that even generals can get fired, but more importantly to emphasize that true leadership does not rely on rank. Take away the rank and position, and what is left is the leader's ability to influence others by who he is inside. Leading with rank is not the mark of a good boss.

WHAT TO DO NOW?

If you enjoyed this book, please head over to Amazon and leave a review. I'd love to hear from you and so would other leaders!

Then go to WWW.THEMILITARYLEADER.COM and subscribe by email to get the latest content when it comes out.

Follow on Twitter (@mil_LEADER) and Facebook (@MilitaryLeader).

Then check out The Military Leader Podcast on iTunes, Spotify, Stitcher, and at WWW.THEMILITARYLEADER.COM/PODCAST.

THANKS FOR READING!